Kathy Schrock's
Every Day of the School Year Series
Using Literature in the Middle School Classroom

by
Nancy J. Keane

LINWORTH
LEARNING

From the Minds of Teachers

To my children, Aureta and Alex Keane and my new grandson, Aiden.
And to the memory of my mother, Aureta C. Keane

Library of Congress Cataloging-in-Publication Data

Keane, Nancy J.
  Using literature in the middle school classroom / Nancy J. Keane.
     p. cm.
  Includes index.
  ISBN 1-58683-182-8 (pbk.)
 1. Reading (Middle school)—United States. 2. Middle school
students—Books and reading—United States. 3. Content area reading. 4.
Interdisciplinary approach in education. I. Title.
LB1632.K44 2005
428.4'071'2—dc22

                                        2004025086

Author: **Nancy J. Keane**

Published by Linworth Publishing, Inc.
480 East Wilson Bridge Road, Suite L
Worthington, Ohio 43085

ISBN: 1-58683-182-8

5 4 3 2 1

Table of Contents

Table of Figures

A Word From Kathy Schrock

Welcome to the Every Day of the School Year Series! As an educator, library media specialist, and now technology administrator, I know how important it is for the classroom teacher to extend the learning experiences in the classroom. With the current focus on standards-based teaching, learning, and assessment, I felt it was important to supply classroom teachers and library media specialists with activities that directly support the curriculum, but, at the same time, allow for creative teachers to provide supplementary and extension activities for their students.

The activities in this series are varied in scope, but all of them provide practical tips, tricks, ideas, activities, and units. Many of the activities include related print and Internet sites that are easily collected by the classroom teacher before engaging in the activity. There are handouts, worksheets, and much more throughout the books, too.

In my job as technology administrator for a school district, I am often able to plan lessons with teachers and visit classrooms to observe the teaching of the lesson. In addition, as the creator and maintainer, since 1995, of Kathy Schrock's Guide for Educators (http://discoveryschool.com/schrockguide/), a portal of categorized Web sites for teachers, I often receive e-mail from teachers who are searching for practical, creative, and easy-to-implement activities for the classroom. I hope this series provides just the impetus for you to stretch and enhance your textbook, lesson, and standards-based unit by use of these activities!

If you have any titles you would like to see added to the series, or would like to author yourself, drop me a note at kathy@kathyschrock.net.

Kathy Schrock, MLS

schrockk@nausetschools.org

Kathy Schrock's Guide for Educators

http://discoveryschool.com/schrockguide/

Administrator for Technology

Nauset Public Schools

78 Eldredge Park Way, Orleans, MA 02653

508-255-0016 x216 (FAX: 508-240-2351)

Acknowledgments

I wish to thank the people who have helped with this endeavor. First, I would like to thank all the authors who give us these marvelous stories to enjoy. With so many children's books in print, it is always difficult to limit the entries. Without these extraordinary people, this would have been a thankless task. As it was, I have spent numerous entertaining hours wrapped up in the books.

I would also like to thank many librarians and teachers. They have introduced me to books I may have missed. The many wonderful, dedicated teachers I have had the privilege of knowing also influenced this work tremendously. Their ideas for activities and their willingness to share have helped a great deal. I have been fortunate to work with a talented group of educators.

I would also like to thank my marvelous editor, Kathy Schrock. She has worked with me from the start of this manuscript offering advice and support. She is truly amazing!

Most importantly, I would like to thank my family. My children Aureta and Alex didn't complain too much about the amount of time I spent in the library or on the computer. They listened to the books I read to them and gave me their opinions on them. If you really want to know if a child will like a book, ask a child. If they grew tired of my spontaneous booktalks, they didn't let on. My children are the best! And now I have a grandchild who is still too young to give me much feedback but I look forward to sharing books with Aiden for years to come.

❖ Introduction ❖

Children's literature has long been a vital part of children's lives. Stories reflect society and help our students learn about their world. Children's literature also shows children different perspectives and allows them to experience events in a non-threatening way. Historical fiction introduces them to what life was like long ago. Literary fiction introduces them to the beauty of language. And children's literature can also present valuable information and ideas about mathematics, science, and other subjects. Fiction makes difficult concepts accessible because it is told in a way that is understandable to young children. By using children's literature to teach young learners, the door is open to expand the exploration of topics more in depth. Using fiction as a component to a lesson also allows teachers to differentiate instruction so students on multiple levels can access materials suitable for their learning abilities.

Many middle schools are organized around the concept of teams in which a group of teachers have the same group of students every day. Their classrooms are clustered together in the same area of the building. The team consists of two or four teachers. Together, teams teach science, language arts, social studies, and mathematics. There are many positive advantages to the team approach during the middle school years. Classrooms that are contiguous make it easier for students to get back and forth to class on time, especially since lockers are located in the team area of the wing. Since team teachers have the same planning period, they are able to plan for curriculum integration, interdisciplinary units, field trips, and special activities for their students. Communication and support among teachers is much greater with this approach. Parent conferences and special education meetings are made easier by the fact that all of a student's content area teachers are available at the same time of the day. Students also feel like they are part of a group when on a team. It creates a "school within a school." The team helps provide the child, who is accustomed to a self-contained classroom, a transition to multiple teachers but in a safe, contained way.

The team approach in the middle school lends itself nicely to teaching concepts in interdisciplinary units. An interdisciplinary unit is one where all the teachers on the team teach around one theme and apply it to the subject. For example, in a unit on travel, the social studies teacher would teach mapping skills, the English teacher would do a research report, the math teacher would teach currency exchange, the reading teacher would provide readings about the countries, and the science teacher would cover the plant and animal life of the various locales. Students are involved with many interdisciplinary units throughout their middle school years. Incorporating a literature component to any interdisciplinary unit is a great way to extend learning to appeal to a diverse academic group.

Adding a fiction component to single-subject lessons is also a great way to extend learning. Students can use fiction to broaden their understanding of topics in all subjects and apply what they have learned. For instance, students studying The Renaissance can read fiction set during that time and better understand what they are learning. Students who are studying geography can read a fiction book featuring a journey and be able to track the character's movements. Students studying immigration can read fiction about immigrant experiences, which gives them a character to care about.

The purpose of this book is to promote fiction reading and to encourage the discussion to go further into real life activities. The emphasis is on the middle school curriculum. The themes examined are those typically explored during the middle school years. A sample booktalk, a lesson plan, a list of books that illustrate the theme, and suggested Web sites for further exploration accompany most themes.

The booktalks are short teasers to get the children interested in the books. These can be modified to reflect the needs of the population of children and the style of the booktalker.

Most books included have been published since the year 2000. I have included older material to enhance some of the newer selections when it seemed appropriate to do so. Information given about each book includes the following: author, title, publisher, date of publication, interest level (IL – given as grade level), reading level if known (RL – given as grade level), and the number of pages. In addition, a short annotation based on the Library of Congress summary statement is given. There is a wide range of reading levels and interests represented in this book. In order to facilitate the differentiation of instruction, there are many interest levels and readiness levels to choose from.

Activities and/or discussion topics are included with each booktalk. These activities are suggestions of the type of things you may want to do with your students in order to follow up on the theme. They are just starters and leave plenty of room for you to personalize the activity.

It is hoped that teachers, school librarians, and public librarians will find inspiration in this book to use fiction books as a starting point for the discussion of themes. When children begin a lesson with enthusiasm, it's sure to be a hit.

To find out more about booktalking and to access a database of ready-to-use booktalks, visit the author's Web page *Booktalks—Quick and Simple* at <http://www.nancykeane.com>. The author has also set up a Listserv to share and discuss booktalks. To join, simply visit *Booktalks—Quick and Simple* and click on "Join Booktalkers Group" or go to <http://groups.yahoo.com/group/booktalkers/>.

CHAPTER 1

Genre Studies

Alphabet Books

Alphabet books can be used in any subject area. There are alphabet books about science, history, and even math! Having students create an alphabet book as a final project is a fun way to teach content area vocabulary, and students can demonstrate they have a firm grasp on content when they create an alphabet book.

Sample Booktalk:

Allen, Susan, 1951. *Read Anything Good Lately?* Millbrook Press, 2003, IL K-3, RL 3.7, 32p

Where do you read? Have you read anything good lately? This unique alphabet book shows lots of great places to read and lots of great things to read. What about gossip in the grocery line, or tall tales in my tree house? When you've finished this book, I just bet you'll think of lots of places to read!

Create Your Own Alphabet Book

Making an alphabet book on any topic is a fun learning experience for students of all ages and abilities. The idea can be utilized in many subjects to help students learn a topic through research, drawing, and the production of a finished product.

As a result of this activity, the students will be very familiar with their topic and will have used some thinking skills, research skills, art skills, and cooperative skills.

Students should have access to a variety of alphabet books or access to library, dictionaries, encyclopedias, paper, pencil, crayons, or other media.

Activities and Procedures:

1. Look at several alphabet books. Brainstorm commonalities among these books. Have students develop a rubric of the components of an alphabet book.

2. Assign letters of the alphabet to individuals, partners, or groups.

3. Do research, if need be, to find the core word for the page. Brainstorming could be done for this.

4. Create a sentence for the page that includes a noun, verb, adjective, and adverb plus other words if wanted. Brainstorm and do research to find these.

5. Design a page for the book putting as many pictures of items beginning with that letter as appropriate plus the sentence.

The final books can be shared among the class or even shared with younger students.

Alphabet Book List

The Dog from Arf! Arf! to Zzzzzz. HarperCollins Publishers, 2004, IL K-3, 40p
Annotation missing

Allen, Susan, 1951. *Read Anything Good Lately?* Millbrook Press, 2003, IL K-3, RL 3.7, 32p
An alphabetical look at some different places and things to read, from an atlas at the airport to a zodiac at the zoo.

Azarian, Mary. *A Gardener's Alphabet*. Houghton Mifflin, 2000, IL K-3, RL 1.5, 32p
An alphabet book featuring words associated with gardening, including bulbs, compost, digging, insects, and weeds.

Bonder, Dianna. *Accidental Alphabet*. Whitecap Books, 2002, IL K-3, RL 4.8, 32p
Illustrations and rhymes about a jumble of accident-prone characters introduce each letter of the alphabet. Includes clues to finding hidden letters and objects.

Bronson, Linda. *The Circus Alphabet*. Henry Holt, 2001, IL K-3, RL 1.1, 34p
Simple rhyming text and illustrations present some aspect of the circus for each letter from A to Z.

Bunting, Eve, 1928. *Girls: A to Z*. Boyds Mills Press, 2002, IL K-3, RL 2.8, 32p
Girls with names ranging from Aliki to Zoe imagine themselves in various fun and creative professions.

Catalanotto, Peter. *Matthew A.B.C.* Atheneum Books for Young Readers, 2002, IL K-3, RL 6.0, 32p
A new boy named Matthew joins Mrs. Tuttle's class, which already has twenty-five students whose first names are Matthew and whose last names begin with every letter except Z.

Cheney, Lynne V. *America: A Patriotic Primer*. Simon & Schuster Books for Young Readers, 2002, IL K-3, RL 4.4, 40p
Each letter of the alphabet is represented by important people, ideas, and events in the history of the United States.

Chesworth, Michael. *Alphaboat*. Farrar, Straus and Giroux, 2002, IL K-3, RL 4.2, 32p
Rhyming text full of puns tells the story of the letters of the alphabet sailing off to look for a buried treasure.

Demarest, Chris L. *Firefighters A to Z*. Margaret K. McElderry, 2000, IL K-3, RL 2.2, 32p
An alphabetic look at a firefighter's day.

Edwards, Wallace. *Alphabeasts*. Kids Can Press, 2002, IL K-3, RL 3.2, 32p
Introduces the letters of the alphabet through short verses about the animal inhabitants of a remarkable old house.

Fleming, Denise, 1950. *Alphabet Under Construction*. Henry Holt, 2002, IL K-3, RL 2.4, 32p
A mouse works his way through the alphabet as he folds the "F," measures the "M," and rolls the "R."

Frampton, David. *My Beastie Book of ABC: Rhymes and Woodcuts*. HarperCollins, 2002, IL K-3, RL 3.7, 32p
Illustrations and brief rhymes present an alphabet of animals from alligator and hippo to parrot and zebra.

Grassby, Donna. *A Seaside Alphabet*. Tundra Books of Northern New York, 2000, IL K-3, RL 5.1, 32p
Teaches young readers the alphabet by means of simple text and pictures of the coasts of Maine, Nova Scotia, and Prince Edward Island.

Grimes, Nikki. *C Is for City*. Wordsong/Boyds Mills Press, 2002, IL K-3, RL 3.9, 40p
Rhyming verses describe different aspects of life in a city, featuring each letter of the alphabet. Includes a complete list of all objects and actions featured in the illustrations, which begin with the particular letter of the alphabet.

Isadora, Rachel. *On Your Toes: A Ballet A B C*. Greenwillow Books, 2003, IL K-3, RL 0.9, 32p
Each letter of the alphabet is represented by an illustration of a ballet-related word.

Jay, Alison. ABC: *A Child's First Alphabet Book*. Dutton Children's Books, 2003, IL K-3, RL 1.6, 32p
In this alphabet book, A is for apple and Z is for zoo.

Kratter, Paul. *The Living Rain Forest: An Animal Alphabet*. Charlesbridge, 2004, IL K-3, RL 5.8, 57p
Introduces 26 rain forest animals from A to Z, providing the name, favorite foods, and unique characteristics of each.

Krull, Kathleen. *M Is for Music*. Harcourt, 2003, IL K-3, RL 4.3, 48p
An alphabet book introducing musical terms, from allegro to zarzuela.

Lester, Mike. *A Is for Salad*. Putnam & Grosset, 2000, IL K-3, RL 2.5, 32p
Each letter of the alphabet is presented in an unusual way, such as: "A is for salad" showing an alligator eating a bowl of greens.

Macdonald, Ross. *Achoo! Bang! Crash!: The Noisy Alphabet*. Roaring Brook Press, 2003, IL K-3, 32p
Words about sound and noise illustrate the letters of the alphabet.

Melmed, Laura Krauss. *Capital!: Washington D.C. from A to Z*. HarperCollins, 2003, IL K-3, RL 4.4, 42p
Rhyming text and illustrations present the sights of Washington, D.C, from A to Z.

Milich, Zoran. *The City ABC Book*. *Kids Can Press*, 2001, IL K-3, RL 1.0, 32p
Photos demonstrate the surprising places where the letters of the alphabet can be found outdoors in the city.

Murphy, Mary, 1961. *The Alphabet Keeper*. Alfred A. Knopf, Distributed by Random House, 2003, 2002, IL K-3, RL 2.3, 28p
The Alphabet Keeper keeps all the letters caged in the dark, but one day they escape and use clever word play to outwit the keeper.

Pallotta, Jerry. *The Skull Alphabet Book*. Charlesbridge, 2002, IL K-3, RL 4.5, 32p
Asks the reader to identify, by learning functions of facial bones and teeth, the skull of an animal for each letter of the alphabet.

Rash, Andy. *Agent A to Agent Z*. Arthur A. Levine Books, 2004, IL K-3, RL 5.1, 34p
A spy named Agent A inspects his fellow spies, all similarly named after letters of the alphabet.

Saffer, Barbara. *ABC Science Riddles*. Peel Productions, 2001, IL 3-6, RL 1.7, 32p
Presents color-illustrated rhyming riddles, one for each letter of the alphabet, that teach about astronomy, chemistry, geology, biology, and other fields of science.

Schwartz, David M. *Q Is for Quark: A Science Alphabet Book.* Tricycle Press, 2001, IL 5-8, RL 8.0, 64p
Discusses 26 scientific concepts, one for each letter of the alphabet.

Scillian, Devin. *A Is for America: An American Alphabet.* Sleeping Bear Press, 2001, IL 3-6, RL 3.5, 56p
Features a brief rhyme for each letter of the alphabet that provides information about some aspect of America.

Shahan, Sherry. *The Jazzy Alphabet.* Philomel Books, 2002, IL K-3, RL 4.5, 32p
The jazzy alphabet boogies and sings, making hot, cool, pizzazzy, street-jammin' jazz.

Sobel, June. *B Is for Bulldozer: A Construction ABC.* Harcourt, 2003, IL K-3, RL 2.6, 32p
As children watch over the course of a year, builders construct a roller coaster using tools and materials that begin with each letter of the alphabet.

Troll, Ray, 1954. *Sharkabet: A Sea of Sharks from A to Z.* Westwinds Press, 2002, IL K-3, RL 3.9, 39p
Illustrations and simple text provide an alphabetically arranged profile of the many different kinds of sharks.

Wethered, Peggy. *Touchdown Mars!: An ABC Adventure.* G. P. Putnam, 2000, IL K-3, RL 2.6, 36p
An alphabet book that presents facts about a space expedition to Mars.

Wisnewski, Andrea. *A Cottage Garden Alphabet.* D. Godine, 2002, IL K-3, RL 1.5, 62p
Pictures and text associate some aspect of cottage gardening with each letter of the alphabet.

Wood, Audrey. *Alphabet Adventure.* Blue Sky Press, 2001, IL K-3, RL 2.1, 32p
On their way to school, the little letters of the alphabet have to rescue little "i" and then find his dot before they can proceed.

Wood, Audrey. *Alphabet Mystery.* Blue Sky Press, 2003, IL K-3, RL 3.7, 32p
Little x is missing from Charley's Alphabet, and the other lowercase letters go off to solve the mystery of his disappearance, learning in the end how valuable a little x can be.

Wordless Picture Books

Wordless picture books offer students a great way to understand the relationship of words to pictures. Students must interpret the author's story by using inference. Students can use their own background knowledge to interpret the stories in a variety of ways.

Sample Booktalk:

Liu, Jae Soo. *Yellow Umbrella*. Kane/Miller, 2002, IL K-3, 32p

On a rainy day, do you carry an umbrella? Do you feel all safe and cozy inside the umbrella? Does it make you feel alone and lonely? This book takes you on a journey with a yellow umbrella. The book comes with a music CD. Listen to the music as you look at the pages and get carried away with the Yellow Umbrella.

Interpreting Wordless Picture Books

In this lesson, students will explore the genre by reading a variety of wordless picture books. They will work in pairs to develop an oral story line for the book. Students can share this story with the class. Next, have the students work to create an alternative story line using the same picture book. Using photocopies or scans of the pages, have students work together to write the alternative story line.

This activity can be used in any subject area. Have the students create a story using the same book to explain a scientific principle, an historical event, or even a mathematical concept.

Wordless Picture Book List

Anno, Mitsumasa, 1926. *Anno's Spain*. Philomel Books, 2004, 2003, IL K-3, 48p
Wordless illustrations depict the cities and historical eras of Spain.

Baker, Jeannie. *Home*. Greenwillow Books, 2004, IL K-3, 32p
A wordless picture book that observes the changes in a neighborhood from before a girl is born until she is an adult, as it first decays and then is renewed by the efforts of the residents.

Bang, Molly. *The Grey Lady and the Strawberry Snatcher*. Four Winds Press, 1986, 1980, IL K-3, 48p
The strawberry snatcher tries to wrest the strawberries from the grey lady, but as he follows her through shops and woods he discovers some delicious blackberries instead.

Carmi, Giora. *A Circle of Friends*. Star Bright Books, 2003, IL K-3, 32p
When a boy anonymously shares his snack with a homeless man, he begins a cycle of good will.

Day, Alexandra. *Good Dog, Carl*. Aladdin Paperbacks, 1997, 1985, IL K-3, 36p
Lively and unusual things happen when Carl the dog is left in charge of the baby.

dePaola, Tomie. *The Hunter and the Animals: A Wordless Picture Book*. Holiday House, 1981, IL K-3, 32p
When the discouraged hunter falls asleep, the forest animals play a trick on him.

Dematons, Charlotte, 1957. *The Yellow Balloon*. Front Street, 2003. IL K-3,
A yellow balloon sails around the world.

Fleischman, Paul. *Sidewalk Circus*. Candlewick Press, 2004, IL K-3, 32p
A young girl watches as the activities across the street from her bus stop become a circus.

Liu, Jae Soo. *Yellow Umbrella*. Kane/Miller, 2002, IL K-3, 32p
Combines a wordless picture book, in which an increasing number of colorful umbrellas appear in the falling rain, with a CD of background music designed to enrich the images.

Louchard, Antonin. *Little Star*. Hyperion Books for Children, 2003, IL K-3, 48p
A tiny starfish dreams of leaving its ocean home and traveling high up into the dark sky to shine among the celestial stars.

McCully, Emily Arnold. *Four Hungry Kittens*. Dial Books for Young Readers, 2001, IL K-3, 32p
In this wordless story, four kittens share adventures while their mother is away hunting food.

Sis, Peter. *Dinosaur!* Greenwillow Books, 2000, IL K-3, 24p
While taking a bath, a young boy is joined by all sorts of dinosaurs.

Vincent, Gabrielle. *A Day, A Dog*. Front Street, 2000, IL K-3, 64p
Pictures tell the story of a dog's day, from the moment he is abandoned on the highway until he finds a friend in a young boy.

Weitzman, Jacqueline Preiss. *You Can't Take a Balloon into the Museum of Fine Arts*. Dial Books for Young Readers, 2002, IL K-3, 35p
While a brother and sister, along with their grandparents, visit the Museum of Fine Arts, the balloon they were not allowed to bring into the museum floats around Boston, causing a series of mishaps at various tourist sites.

Wiesner, David. *June 29, 1999*. Clarion Books, 1992, IL K-3, 32p
While her third-grade classmates are sprouting seeds in paper cups, Holly has a more ambitious, innovative science project in mind.

Wiesner, David. *Tuesday*. Clarion Books, 1991, IL K-3, 32p
Frogs rise on their lily pads, float through the air, and explore the nearby houses while their inhabitants sleep.

❖ Poetry Books ❖

Poetry can be a powerful tool in story telling. Poetry is meant to be read, heard, and enjoyed. A look at poetry should not overlook novels written in verse. These tell a story about a character. Have students tell their story in a poem.

 ### Sample Booktalk:

Frost, Helen, 1949. *Keesha's House*. Farrar, Straus and Giroux, 2003, IL or RL, 116p

It's really Joe's house. It was left to him with the instructions that he should use it to help others. But everyone thinks of it as Keesha's house. She's the one who finds the kids who need help. She's the one to figure out what they need and assign rooms. She's the one to offer advice and friendship. Sometimes it's hard to believe that she's just a kid herself. A kid in need of a place to live so she can finish school and make something of herself. Other teens find themselves at Keesha's house. Some for just a few nights. Some for longer. But one thing is for sure. They are safe here.

I Am Poem

Begin by describing two things about yourself--special things about yourself. Avoid the obvious and the ordinary such as "I am a 14-year-old boy with brown hair." There are millions of 14-year-old boys with brown hair. Think about the things about yourself that are distinctive.

"I am a girl who bruises easily and believes in astrology--when the stars are right." That is better because it gives a sense of the speaker. And now she is different from other people. Don't be afraid to be different.

Once you have an opening line, you're ready to take off. Here is a line-by-line guide you can follow.

It may seem strange at first to write a poem this way, but give it a try. You may surprise yourself. Some students who have tried this approach have been amazed by the results.

I am (two special characteristics you have).
I wonder (something you are actually curious about).
I hear (an imaginary sound).
I see (an imaginary sight).
I want (an actual desire).
I am (the first line of the poem repeated).

I pretend (something you actually pretend to do).
I feel (a feeling about something imaginary).
I touch (an imaginary touch).
I worry (something that really bothers you).
I cry (something that makes you very sad).
I am (the first line of the poem repeated).

I understand (something you know is true).
I say (something you believe in).
I dream (something you actually dream about).
I try (something for which you really make an effort).
I hope (something you actually hope for).
I am (the first line of the poem repeated).

Poetry Book List

Creech, Sharon. *Love That Dog*. Joanna Cotler Books, 2001. RL 4.1, 86p
A young student, who comes to love poetry through a personal understanding of what different famous poems mean to him, surprises himself by writing his own inspired poem.

Frost, Helen, 1949. *Keesha's House*. Farrar, Straus and Giroux, 2003. IL or RL, 116p
Seven teens facing such problems as pregnancy, closeted homosexuality, and abuse each describe in poetic forms what caused them to leave home and where they found home again.

Glenn, Mel. *Jump Ball: A Basketball Season in Poems*. Lodestar Books, 1997. RL 7.5, 151p
Tells the story of a high school basketball team's season through a series of poems reflecting the feelings of students, their families, teachers, and coaches.

Glenn, Mel. *Who Killed Mr. Chippendale?: A Mystery in Poems*. Puffin, 1999, 1996. RL 6.0, 100p
A murder mystery told in free verse poems, describing the reactions of students, colleagues, and others when high school teacher Mr. Chippendale, loved by some, hated by others, is shot as the school day begins.

Grimes, Nikki. *Bronx Masquerade*. Dial Books, 2002. IL or RL, 167p
While studying the Harlem Renaissance, students at a Bronx high school read aloud poems they've written, revealing their innermost thoughts and fears to their formerly clueless classmates.

Hesse, Karen. *Out of the Dust*. Scholastic Press, 1997, RL 4.5, 227p
In a series of poems, fifteen-year-old Billie Jo relates the hardships of living on her family's wheat farm in Oklahoma during the dust bowl years of the Depression.

Koertge, Ronald. *Shakespeare Bats Cleanup*. Candlewick Press, 2003, IL or RL, 116p
When a fourteen-year-old baseball player catches mononucleosis, he discovers that keeping a journal and experimenting with poetry not only helps fill the time, it also helps him deal with life, love, and loss.

Sones, Sonya. *Stop Pretending: What Happened When My Big Sister Went Crazy*. HarperCollins, 1999. RL 5.0, 149p
A younger sister has a difficult time adjusting to life after her older sister has a mental breakdown.

Wolff, Virginia Euwer. *Make Lemonade*. Scholastic, 1994, 1993, RL 5.2, 200p
In order to earn money for college, fourteen-year-old LaVaughn babysits for a teenage mother.

Web Sites

International Library of Poetry: <http://www.poetry.com>
This site accepts contributions from poets all over the world. There are currently more than 5.1 million poets who are included. Special features also include a rhyming dictionary, information on poetry techniques, and the full text of many of the greatest poems ever written.

The Academy of American Poets: <http://www.poets.org/>
This is a collection of more than 500 poet biographies, 1400 poems, and 100 audio clips. Also includes lesson plans for teaching poetry to students.

J ust what is a multigenre novel? It's a novel told with a variety of genres. There could be poetry and newspaper articles, emails and postcards, or even a little bit of everything. What makes these novels fun is that the story is told in a variety of ways. In this chapter, we look at multigenre novels and then create our own multigenre story.

 ### Sample Booktalk:

Andrews-Goebel, Nancy. *The Pot That Juan Built*. Lee & Low, 2002. IL or RL, 32p

The Mexican village of Mata Ortiz had a tradition of poverty and migrant workers. Juan Quezada has lived in the village most of his life. As a young boy, he spent time exploring and came upon some pottery fragments that were very old. He didn't know it at the time, but he had discovered the remains of pottery from 600 years ago. He studied the pottery and through the years taught himself the art of making this unique pottery. Word of this beautiful pottery spread and now the village is a lively artist village. Just about every household has at least one potter in it. Find out how Juan changed his poor village into a community of world famous artists. Told in a variety of genre.

Multigenre Folder Report

Students will create a folder report. Using a manila file folder, students will report on a topic of their own choosing. It might be sports, music, books, etc.

The folder must include a minimum of five genres. The list below contains suggestions but it is not exhaustive. There are many more that can be used. All four pages of the folder must be used.

Although the report will be written using many different genres, there must be a consistent theme throughout. There can be an introduction that explains the piece or even a narrator throughout. Use your imagination.

What are some genres I might include?

advertisement
application (i.e. for a job)
autobiography
award certificate
business card
choose your own adventure
collage
comic strip
dialogue
editorial
email
eulogy
fairy tale
fantasy
flashback
graffiti
greeting card
illustration
IM conversation
letter
magazine article
memo
memory
newspaper article
obituary
outline
phone conversation
photograph
poem
postcard
pro/con list
ransom note

rap lyrics
recipe
restaurant menu
resume
romance
science fiction
scrapbook page
song
speech
tabloid article
top ten list
travel poster
wanted poster
western

Multigenre Book List

Picture Books and Short Chapter Books:

Andrews-Goebel, Nancy. *The Pot That Juan Built*. Lee & Low, 2002, IL or RL, 32p
Also available in Spanish, *La Vasija Que Juan Fabricó*

Arnold, Katya, with Sam Swope. *Katya's Book of Mushrooms*. Henry Holt, 1997, IL or RL, 48p
Annotation missing

Bang, Molly. *Nobody Particular: One Woman's Fight to Save the Bays*. Henry Holt, 2000, IL or RL, 45p
Annotation missing

Cole, Joanna. *Ms. Frizzle's Adventures: Ancient Egypt*. Scholastic, 2001, IL or RL, 48p
Annotation missing

Coulter, Laurie. *Secrets in Stone: All About Maya Hieroglyphs*. Little, Brown, 2001, IL or RL, 48p
Annotation missing

Dewey, Jennifer Owings. *Rattlesnake Dance*. Boyds Mill Press, 1997, IL or RL, 48p
Annotation missing

Hoyt-Goldsmith, Diane. *Celebrating Ramadan*. Holiday House, 2001, IL or RL, 32p
Annotation missing

Kurlansky, Mark. *The Cod's Tale*. Putnam, 2001, IL or RL, 48p
Annotation missing

Macaulay, David. *Black and White*. Houghton Mifflin, 1990, IL or RL, 32p
Annotation missing

Martin, Jacqueline Briggs. *Snowflake Bentley*. Houghton Mifflin, 1998, IL or RL, 32p
Annotation missing

Longer Works:

Avi. *Nothing but the Truth: A Documentary Novel*. HarperTrophy, 1993, IL or RL, 224p
Annotation missing

Cofer, Judith Ortiz. *The Year of Our Revolution: New and Selected Stories and Poems*. Puffer, 2000, IL or RL, 144p
Annotation missing

Conrad, Pam. *Our House: Stories of Levittown*. Scholastic, 1995, IL or RL, 96p
Annotation missing

Draper, Sharon. *Tears of a Tiger*. Atheneum, 1994, IL or RL, 192p
Annotation missing

Dyson, George B. *Baidarka: The Kayak*. Alaska Northwest Books, 1986, IL or RL, 212p
Annotation missing

Klise, Kate. *Regarding the Fountain: A Tale, in Letters, of Liars and Leaks.* Avon, 1999, IL or RL, 144p
Annotation missing.

Kumar, Amitava. *Passport Photos.* University of California Press, 2000, IL or RL, 276p
Annotation missing

Murphy, Claire Rudolf. *The Prince and the Salmon People.* Rizzoli, 1993, IL or RL, 48p
Annotation missing

Myers, Walter Dean. *Monster.* HarperCollins, 1999, IL or RL, 288p
Annotation missing

Strasser, Todd. *Give a Boy a Gun.* Simon and Schuster, 2000, IL or RL, 208p
Annotation missing

Wittlinger, Ellen. *Hard Love.* Aladdin, 1999, IL or RL, 240p
Annotation missing

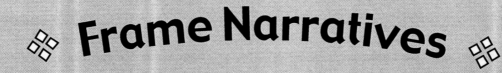

Frame Narratives

A frame narrative is a story within a story, within sometimes yet another story. An individual other than who told the original story often tells the story. This structure leads us to question the reasons behind each of the narrations since the teller of the story becomes an actual character with shortcomings, limitations, prejudices, and motives. Sometimes the narrative is told from several different viewpoints as different characters narrate the same event.

Have students create a simple frame narrative story. The story should have two narrators--one from today and one from the past. Students should use the storyboard to help plan the story.

 ## Sample Booktalk:

Lowry, Lois. *Gooney Bird Greene*. Houghton Mifflin, 2002, IL K-3, RL 5.0, 88p

No one knows what to make of Gooney Bird Greene. She's new in school and tells the teacher right from the start that she wants to be in the middle of everything. She tells them that she just moved to Watertower from China and has lots of stories to tell. Like how they drove all the way from China. Or how she arrived on a flying carpet. Or how a cow consumed her cat. And, she assures them every one of her stories is absolutely true.

Build Your Own Frame Narrative Story

	Present Day Narrator	Past Narrator
Story Element		
Story Element		
Story Element		
Story Element		

Frame Narratives Book List

Base, Graeme. *The Eleventh Hour: A Curious Mystery.* Abrams, 1989, IL 3-6, RL 3.5, 32p
An elephant's 11th birthday party is marked by 11 games preceding the banquet to be eaten at the 11th hour; but when the time to eat arrives, the birthday feast has disappeared. The reader is invited to guess the thief.

Delacre, Lulu. *Salsa Stories.* Scholastic Press, 2000, IL 3-6, RL 5.2, 105p
A collection of stories within the story of a family celebration where the guests relate their memories of growing up in various Latin American countries. Also contains recipes.

Fleming, Candace. *The Hatmaker's Sign: A Story by Benjamin Franklin.* Orchard Books, 2000, 1998, IL K-3, RL 4.2, 36p
To heal the hurt pride of Thomas Jefferson as Congress makes changes to his Declaration of Independence, Benjamin Franklin tells his friend the story of a hatmaker and his sign.

Harley, Bill, 1954. *Sarah's Story.* Tricycle Press, 1996, IL K-3, RL 2.8, 32p
Sarah cannot think of a story to tell in class for her homework assignment, but on her way to school she gets help from some unexpected sources.

Lowry, Lois. *Gooney Bird Greene.* Houghton Mifflin, 2002, IL K-3, RL 5.0, 88p
A most unusual new student who loves to be the center of attention entertains her teacher and fellow second graders by telling absolutely true stories about herself, including how she got her name.

Sendak, Maurice. *In the Night Kitchen.* HarperCollins, 1970, IL K-3, RL 2.8, 40p
A little boy's dream-fantasy in which he helps three fat bakers get milk for their cake batter.

Sunami, Kitoba. *How the Fisherman Tricked the Genie: A Tale Within a Tale Within a Tale.* Atheneum Books for Young Readers, 2002, IL K-3, RL 3.8, 34p
After releasing a captive genie from a bottle, a poor fisherman must rely on his wits when instead of wishes the genie promises revenge.

Waddell, Martin. *A Kitten Called Moonlight.* Candlewick Press, 2001, IL K-3, RL 2.6, 32p
A little girl and her mother recall how a special kitten came into their lives one dark and stormy night.

Wiesner, David. *The Three Pigs.* Clarion Books, 2001, IL K-3, RL 2.4, 40p
The three pigs escape the wolf by going into another world where they meet the cat and the fiddle, the cow that jumped over the moon, and a dragon.

Yolen, Jane. *Merlin and the Dragons.* Puffin Books, 1998, 1995, IL 3-6, RL 5.4, 38p
When young Arthur is troubled by dreams, Merlin tells him a story about a fatherless boy who himself dreamed about dragons and the defeat of the evil king Vortigern.

Based on a True Story

"Ripped from Today's Headlines!"

There is a television show that proclaims that the storylines are "ripped from today's headlines." These stories are based on actual events but the details have been changed a bit to make them fit the format of the show. There are many books that take events from the headlines and fictionalize the story. In this chapter, students will be reading novels ripped from the headlines and then create their own.

Sample Booktalk:

Watts, Irene N. *Finding Sophie*. Tundra Books of Northern New York, 2002, IL 5-8, RL 6.7, 136p

Sophie is only seven years old and can't understand what is happening around her. How could she when even the adults can't quite understand. All they know is that it is not safe to be a Jew in Germany under Hitler's regime. So Sophie's parents send her to England to live with a friend. Sophie has a good life in spite of the war that is raging around her. Over time she forgets how to speak German and the memories of her parents fade. When the war is finally over, things change for Sophie in ways she never anticipated. People assume that she will go home to Germany. But, for a girl who has spent half her life in this place, England feels more like home to her. Can she really be expected to go back to a country she doesn't remember? And what if her parents didn't survive the war? What will happen to her? Will anyone understand that she wants to stay? This is based on the author's own childhood journeys.

Ripped from Today's Headlines

Create your own story based on a newspaper article. Begin your project by finding an interesting news article on which to base your story. Analyze your news story using the following criteria:

Use complete sentences when answering the following questions. Remember to capitalize and use appropriate punctuation.

■ Who or what is the article about?

■ Explain the main topic. Be sure to include lots of details and a summary of important facts.

■ When and where did it happen? Be specific.

■ What is your opinion and reaction to the topic?

■ How will this topic affect you now or in the future?

Based on a True Story Book List

Alder, Elizabeth. *Crossing the Panther's Path*. Farrar, Straus and Giroux, 2002, IL 5-8, RL 8.1, 229p
Sixteen-year-old Billy Calder, son of a British soldier and a Mohawk woman, leaves school to join Tecumseh in his efforts to prevent the Americans from taking any more land from the Indians in the Northwest Territory.

Crowe, Chris. *Mississippi Trial, 1955*. P. Fogelman Books, 2002, IL 5-8, RL 5.1, 231p
In Mississippi in 1955, a 16-year-old finds himself at odds with his grandfather over issues surrounding the kidnapping and murder of a 14-year-old African-American from Chicago.

Fama, Elizabeth. *Overboard*. Cricket Books, 2002, IL YA, 158p
Escaping from a sinking ferry in the waters off Sumatra, 14-year-old Emily fights for survival for herself and a young Indonesian boy, who draws courage from his quiet but firm Islamic faith.

Konigsburg, E. L. *Silent to the Bone*. Atheneum Books for Young Readers, 2000, IL 5-8, RL 6.0, 261p
Thirteen-year-old Branwell loses his power of speech after being wrongly accused of gravely injuring his baby half-sister, and only his friend Connor is able to reach him and uncover the truth about what happened.

Levitin, Sonia, 1934. *Dream Freedom*. Harcourt, 2000, IL 5-8, RL 5.2, 178p
Marcus and his classmates learn about the terrible problem of slavery in present-day Sudan and raise money to help buy the freedom of some of the slaves. Alternate chapters tell the stories of the slaves.

Lyons, Mary E. *Dear Ellen Bee: A Civil War Scrapbook of Two Union Spies*. Atheneum Books for Young Readers, 2000, IL 5-8, RL 5.9, 161p
A scrapbook kept by a young black girl details her experiences and those of the older white woman, "Miss Bet," who had freed her and her family, sent her north from Richmond to get an education, and then worked to bring an end to slavery. Based on the life of Elizabeth Van Lew.

Ryan, Pam Munoz. *Esperanza Rising*. Scholastic, 2000, IL 5-8, RL 6.2, 262p
Esperanza and her mother are forced to leave their life of wealth and privilege in Mexico to go work in the labor camps of Southern California, where they must adapt to the harsh circumstances facing Mexican farm workers on the eve of the Great Depression.

Strasser, Todd. *Give a Boy a Gun*. Simon & Schuster Books for Young Readers, 2000, IL 5-8, RL 6.4, 146p
Interweaves the voices of students, teachers, friends, and gunmen in a fictional story about two heavily armed students, Gary and Brendan, who hold their classmates hostage at a high school dance after being tormented by football players and teachers. Includes real-life statistics on guns and violence.

Watts, Irene N. *Finding Sophie*. Tundra Books of Northern New York, 2002, IL 5-8, RL 6.7, 136p
Sophie does not know if she belongs in postwar England or with the parents she left behind in Germany.

Wulffson, Don L. *Soldier X*. Viking, 2001, IL 5-8, RL 6.7, 226p
In 1943 sixteen-year-old Erik experiences the horrors of war when he is drafted into the German army and sent to fight on the Russian front.

Current News Web Sites

CNN News:
<http://www.cnn.com>
Annotation missing

Fox News:
<http://www.foxnews.com>
Annotation missing

Washington Post:
<http://www.washingtonpost.com/>
Annotation missing

CHAPTER 2

Social
Studies

Alternative History

It's always fun to think about alternatives to events. What if...? What if the British had won the Revolutionary War? What if you could go back in history and change things? In this chapter, we will be looking at some "What if" books and reading alternative history.

Sample Booktalk:

Etchemendy, Nancy. *The Power of Un*. Front Street/Cricket Books, 2000, IL 5-8, RL 6.6, 148p

Have you ever thought about going back in time? Maybe you've done something stupid and would like to go back and undo what you've done. Wouldn't it be great if there were a way to do that? Maybe a computer game that lets you go back and correct your mistakes. That would be so cool. And Gib Finney can do just that. He has an Unner that allows him to undo what he's done. Life is good! But then there is an accident and Gib can't figure out just what needs to be undone to prevent the tragedy. Was it something minor like the spitball he shot in class? Or maybe the argument he had about the science project. Gib must relive that horrible night over and over again until he can find just the right thing to undo. Or maybe there are things that just can't be undone.

Create Your Own Alternative History

Choose one of the alternative history projects below. Record your choice on the back of this sheet.

1. Illustrate the history
- Using one of the books supplied, read a book of your choice
- Rewrite a significant part of the history in your own words and create illustrations to go along with the text
- Your final project will be a neatly published picture or comic book
- Minimum of ten pages
- Neatly and creatively hand drawn
- Neatly written or word processed
- Create a cover

2. Write your own alternative history
- Use your imagination to write your own alternative history
- Your history must be based on an actual event
- Include at least one "real person" in your history
- Your history may also include any of the following
  - An unlikely event
  - Rewards and/or punishments
  - A moral

3. Put yourself in history
- Use your imagination to put yourself into your alternative history
- Create an alternative history which includes:
  - One or more of your abilities or strengths
  - At least one "real" historical person
  - Your character must influence the changing of history
- Your final project will be a neatly published picture or comic book
- Minimum of ten pages
- Neatly and creatively hand drawn
- Neatly written or word processed

4. Rewrite an alternative history
- Select one of the books suggested from the reading list
- Decide what story elements you would like to change—the ending, the characters, descriptive language, the setting, etc.
- Rewrite the story with your changes
- Your final product shoul be neatly written or word processed

Alternative History Book List

Aiken, Joan. *The Wolves of Willoughby Chase*. Dell, 1987, 1962, IL 5-8, RL 5.6, 168p
Surrounded by villains of the first order, brave Bonnie and gentle cousin Sylvia conquer all obstacles in this Victorian melodrama.

Blackwood, Gary L. *The Year of the Hangman*. Dutton Children's Books, 2002, IL YA, 261p
In 1777, having been kidnapped and taken forcibly from England to the American colonies, 15-year-old Creighton becomes part of developments in the political unrest there that may spell defeat for the patriots and change the course of history.

Card, Orson Scott. *Seventh Son*. Tor, 1988, IL YA, 241p
In an alternate frontier America, Alvin, the seventh son of a seventh son, is born with a destiny to become something great, perhaps even a Maker.

Dickson, Gordon R. *The Dragon and the George*. Ballantine Books, 1976, IL AD, 279p
When an astral projection experiment goes awry and his fiancé disappears, Jim Eckert jumps into the ether after her and finds himself in the body of a dragon.

Etchemendy, Nancy. *The Power of Un*. Front Street/Cricket Books, 2000, IL 5-8, RL 6.6, 148p
When he is given a device that will allow him to "undo" what has happened in the past, Gib Finney is not sure what event from the worst day in his life he should change in order to keep his sister from being hit by a truck.

Flint, Eric. *Fortune's Stroke*. Baen, Distributed by Simon & Schuster, 2000, IL YA, 402p
When a supercomputer from the future threatens to destroy the world, the armies of Good and Evil gather on the plains of Mesopotamia to decide the fate and the future of the world.

Myers, Bill, 1953. *Eli: A Novel*. Zondervan, 2000, IL YA, 349p
After a fiery car crash, television journalist Conrad Davis finds himself transported to an alternate universe where life is exactly the same, except for the fact that Jesus was not born 2,000 years earlier, but was instead born in contemporary society.

Turtledove, Harry. *The Great War: Breakthroughs*. Random House, 2001, 2000, IL YA, 584p
Offers an alternative history of World War II that theorizes how the war would have ended if certain events had been different.

Turtledove, Harry. *The Guns of the South: A Novel of the Civil War*. Ballantine Books, 1997, 1992, IL YA, 513p
An alternate history in which the course of the Civil War is changed by the arrival of a man from the year 2013 who offers to supply General Lee and the Confederacy with AK-47 rifles.

Turtledove, Harry. *Worldwar: Upsetting the Balance*. Ballantine Books, 1996, IL AD, 530p
An alternative history in which the combatants of World War II must unite against a greater enemy from outer space and race to develop weapons and tactics to counter the alien attacks.

Web Site

The Alternative History Web Site:
<http://www.thwww.com/mrwizard/wizardAH.HTM>

Utopia/Dystopia

Throughout history, people have been searching for the perfect life. Many attempts have been made to create a utopian society. A utopia is defined as an ideally perfect place, especially in its social, political, and moral aspects. From Walden to Waco, these societies have sprung up in many parts of the world and for many different purposes. Sometimes these efforts have failed to the point that the societies become dystopias--imaginary places or states in which the condition of life is extremely bad, as from deprivation, oppression, or terror.

 ### Sample Booktalk:

Lowry, Lois. *Messenger.* Houghton Mifflin, 2004, IL YA, 169p

Life in the Village is about to change. Matty has been living with the blind man known as Seer for several years now. Matty had come to the Village as a wild young boy, but has since grown into a fine young man. That's the way of the Village. People who are outcasts in their own homes are welcome with open arms in the Village. The schoolteacher whose face is covered with a birthmark. The blind man. A wild boy. The lame, the weak. All are welcome. But things have been changing lately. People have been changing. Now they want to close the Village. They want no more strangers coming in. Matty and Seer do not understand what is going on but they know it is serious. And they are determined to bring Seer's daughter, Kira into the Village before it is closed forever.

Living in Paradise?

Students will research a utopian society and compare the goals and outcomes to those in the novel they have read.

List of Sites:

1. New Harmony, Indiana:
<http://www.in.gov/ism/HistoricSites/NewHarmony/historic.asp>

2. Pleasant Hill, Kentucky:
<http://www.shakervillageky.org/>

3. Amana, Iowa:
<http://www.amanacolonies.com/educat/low_educat.html>

4. Nauvoo, Illinois:
<http://www.nauvoonet.com/icarians.htm>

5. Twin Oaks:
<http://www.twinoaks.org/>

6. Bronson Alcott's Fruitlands:
<http://www.fruitlands.org/>

Concluding Assignment:

Students will write a short expository essay in which they discuss what they have learned about utopian societies.

Utopia/Dystopia Book List

Bardi, Abby. *The Book of Fred.* Washington Square Press, 2001, IL AD, 292p
A sheltered 15-year-old girl named Mary Fred Anderson is removed from her home in a fundamentalist sect and placed in foster care in a Washington, D.C. suburb. While there a violent act upon her new family has an indelible impact on her, making her reexamine her long-held beliefs.

Beale, Fleur. *I Am Not Esther.* Hyperion, 2002, 1998, IL YA, 250p
After her mother unexpectedly leaves her with her uncle's family, members of a fanatical Christian cult, Kirby tries to learn what has become of her mother and struggles to cope with the repressiveness of her new surroundings and to maintain her own identity.

Blacker, Terence. *The Angel Factory.* Simon & Schuster Books for Young Readers, 2002, IL 5-8, RL 6.6, 216p
Spurred on by his best friend, 12-year-old Thomas uncovers two major family secrets: that he was adopted, and that his perfect-seeming family is part of an otherworldly organization.

Farmer, Nancy, 1941. *The House of the Scorpion*. Atheneum Books for Young Readers, 2002, IL 5-8, RL 6.3, 380p
In a future where humans despise clones, Matt enjoys special status as the young clone of El Patron, the 142-year-old leader of a corrupt drug empire nestled between Mexico and the United States.

Golding, William, 1911. *Lord of the Flies*. Berkley, 2003, 1954, IL YA, 315p
After a plane crash strands them on a tropical island while the rest of the world is ravaged by war, a group of British schoolboys attempts to form a civilized society but descends into brutal anarchy.

Haddix, Margaret Peterson. *Among the Hidden*. Simon & Schuster Books for Young Readers, 1998, IL 3-6, RL 4.7, 153p
In a future where the Population Police enforce the law limiting a family to only two children, Luke has lived all his 12 years in isolation and fear on his family's farm, until another "third" convinces him that the government is wrong.

Huxley, Aldous, 1894-1963. *Brave New World*. Perennial Classics, 1998, 1932, IL YA, 268p
A satirical novel about the utopia of the future, a world in which babies are decanted from bottles and the great Ford is worshipped.

Layne, Steven L. *This Side of Paradise*. Pelican Books, 2001, IL YA, 215p
After his father begins working for the mysterious Eden Corporation, Jack uncovers a sinister plot that threatens the existence of his entire family.

Lowry, Lois. *Gathering Blue*. Houghton Mifflin, 2000, IL 5-8, RL 6.3, 215p
Lame and suddenly orphaned, Kira is mysteriously removed from her squalid village to live in the palatial Council Edifice, where she is expected to use her gifts as a weaver to do the bidding of the all-powerful Guardians.

Lowry, Lois. *The Giver*. Bantam, 1999, 1993, IL 5-8, RL 6.8, 180p
Given his lifetime assignment at the Ceremony of Twelve, Jonas becomes the receiver of memories shared by only one other in his community and discovers the terrible truth about the society in which he lives.

Lowry, Lois. *Messenger*. Houghton Mifflin, 2004, IL YA, 169p
In this novel that unites characters from "The Giver" and "Gathering Blue," Matty, a young member of a utopian community that values honesty, conceals an emerging healing power that he cannot explain or understand.

Nelson, O. T. *The Girl Who Owned a City*. Runestone Press, 1995, IL 5-8, RL 5.1, 200p
When a plague sweeps over the earth killing everyone except children under 12, ten-year-old Lisa organizes a group to rebuild a new way of life.

Orwell, George, 1903-1950. *1984: A Novel*. Signet Classic, 1949, 1977, IL YA, RL 8.2, 268p
Depicts life in a totalitarian regime of the future.

Philbrick, W. R. (W. Rodman). *The Last Book in the Universe*. Blue Sky Press, 2000, IL 5-8, RL 6.0, 223p
After an earthquake has destroyed much of the planet, an epileptic teenager nicknamed Spaz begins the heroic fight to bring human intelligence back to the Earth of a distant future.

Swift, Jonathan, 1667-1745. *Gulliver's Travels*. Grosset & Dunlap, 1947, IL 5-8, RL 8.8, 331p
An Englishman's voyages carry him to Lilliput, a land of people six inches high, and to Brobdingnag, a land of giants.

Ancient Civilizations

The study of ancient civilizations is a favorite among middle school children as they study ancient cultures in the curriculum. Be it the Egyptian mummies or the Roman gladiators, there is something for everyone.

 ## Sample Booktalk:

Lawrence, Caroline. *The Secrets of Vesuvius (The Roman Mysteries)*. Roaring Brook Press, 2002, IL 5-8, RL 7.6, 173p

Flavia, Jonathan, Nubia, and Lupus are back. This time they are trying to solve a riddle for a great scholar. They have had the privilege of meeting Pliny himself and now have a mission. Pliny has seen a riddle posted in a blacksmith shop in the port city of Pompeii. The children are on their way to stay at Flavia's uncle's home near Pompeii. They haven't been looking forward to spending time away but now they have a mystery to solve. Solving the riddle is said to lead to a treasure! So, when they get to Pompeii, they must look up the blacksmith and try to solve the riddle. What they can't know is the danger they are heading into. Quiet Mount Vesuvius is about to lead to a disaster. What will happen to the children? Will they be able to solve the riddle?

An Ancient Civilizations Menu

Of the 12 options listed in the menu, you must complete a minimum of five—at least one for each civilization. Circle the numbers of the questions you have chosen to answer. See the rubric for more information. Each answer must be written in complete sentences. Number the answers to correspond with the questions.

Ancient
Civilizations
Menu

1. List five different areas where people worked.	**2.** What are some of the similarities between you and a child from this civilization? What are some of the major differences?
3. Give examples of a woman's role in this civilization.	**4.** What type of government ruled the civilization?
5. What religion did the civilization practice? Name some of the gods.	**6.** Did the civilization have a written language? Describe it.
7. Describe the educational system. Who were allowed to be educated?	**8.** Describe the climate. What are some of the major geological features?
9. What were some of the major figures of the time? What were the contributions that this person made?	**10.** What role did the military play in the civilization? Who were the soldiers?
11. Was slavery practiced by the civilization? Who were the slaves?	**12.** Name a famous author from your civilization. What did that person write?

An Ancient Civilization Menu Rubric

Read the rubric carefully before beginning your project.

Ancient
Civilizations
Menu

4	<ul><li>Five or more activities completed</li><li>All spelling and punctuation correct</li><li>All pages appropriately numbered</li><li>The cover page is visually attractive and complete with name, date, title, and picture</li><li>All pages neatly done and the finished product is exemplary</li><li>All sources used are cited in MLA format</li></ul>
3	<ul><li>Four or more activities completed</li><li>Most spelling and punctuation correct</li><li>All pages appropriately numbered</li><li>The cover page is visually attractive and complete with name, date, title, and picture</li><li>The finished product is neat</li><li>All sources used are cited</li></ul>
2	<ul><li>Three or more activities completed</li><li>Some spelling and punctuation mistakes</li><li>Most pages are appropriately numbered</li><li>The cover page needs more effort</li><li>Pages should have been rewritten before turned in</li><li>Some of the sources used are listed</li></ul>
1	<ul><li>Two or fewer activities completed</li><li>Many spelling and punctuation mistakes</li><li>Some pages are appropriately numbered</li><li>The cover page is incomplete or missing</li><li>Work presented in an unacceptable condition</li><li>Sources used for research are not included</li></ul>

Ancient Civilizations Book List

Curry, Jane Louise. *The Egyptian Box*. Margaret K. McElderry Books, 2002, IL 3-6, RL 4.4, 186p
Tee is happy to find that the ancient Egyptian box she inherits holds a spirit who will serve her, until she notices changes in her servant's appearance and behavior.

Gregory, Kristiana. *Cleopatra VII: Daughter of the Nile*. Scholastic, 1999, IL 5-8, RL 5.6, 221p
While her father is in hiding after attempts on his life, 12-year-old Cleopatra records in her diary how she fears for her own safety and hopes to survive to become Queen of Egypt some day.

Hunt, Angela Elwell, 1957. *Dreamers*. Bethany House Publishers, 1996, IL YA, 395p
Tuya is a slave in the house of Potiphar. She and another slave, Joseph, become close and dream of a better life and of love, until they are torn apart when Joseph is thrown in prison.

Jacq, Christian. *Nefer the Silent: Volume I*. Pocket books, 2000, IL YA, 400p
Nefer, the son of a village elder in ancient Egypt, must stop the bitter Mehy's attempt to infiltrate the Place of Truth, where an enclave of craftsmen commissioned by Ramses the Great hold the Stone of Light.

Johnston, Tony, 1942. *The Mummy's Mother*. Blue Sky Press, 2003, IL 3-6, RL 5.7, 160p
When his mother is stolen from her tomb, Ramose, a 4000-year-old mummy, tries to find her in the Egyptian desert, aboard an ocean liner, and in New York City's Metropolitan Museum.

Lester, Julius. *Pharaoh's Daughter: A Novel of Ancient Egypt*. Silver Whistle/Harcourt, Inc, 2000, IL YA, 182p
A fictionalized account of a Biblical story in which an Egyptian princess rescues a Hebrew infant who becomes a prophet of his people while his sister finds her true self as a priestess to the Egyptian gods.

Marston, Elsa. *The Ugly Goddess*. Cricket Books, 2002, IL 3-6, RL 6.5, 218p
Fourteen-year-old Princess Meret is unhappy with her future as consort of the Egyptian god Amun, especially after meeting Hector, a handsome Greek soldier, but when she is kidnapped, it is up to Hector and a young servant boy to help rescue her with the aid of the goddess Taweret.

McCaughrean, Geraldine. *Casting the Gods Adrift: A Tale of Ancient Egypt*. Cricket Books, 2002, 1998, IL 5-8, RL 6.4, 103p
Tutmose, an apprentice sculptor, and his nearly-blind brother, Ibrim, an apprentice musician, are content at the court of Pharaoh Akhenaten, but their father rages against Pharaoh's rejection of traditional Egyptian gods and plots a deadly revenge.

Rubalcaba, Jill. *The Wadjet Eye*. Clarion Books, 2000, IL 5-8, RL 6.2, 156p
After his mother dies, Damon, a young medical student living in Alexandria, Egypt, in 45 B.C, makes a perilous journey to Spain to locate his father who is serving in the Roman army led by Julius Caesar.

Greek Mythology

The ancient Greeks had a wonderful way of explaining their world. They had an elaborate mythology that explained every thing from the creation of the world to natural phenomenon. The myths have survived to this day and their influence is quite prevalent in our society. Middle school students love studying the Greek myths and can relate them to their own lives. In this chapter, we examine some modern retellings of traditional Greek myths.

Sample Booktalk:

Spinner, Stephanie. *Quiver*. Knopf, Distributed by Random House, 2002, IL or RL, 177p

Atalanta is a skilled archer and runner. She can outshoot and outrun just about anyone in area. Abandoned at birth, she has been raised by hunters and has learned her lessons well. She believes that the goddess Artemis protected her and saved her life. Now, Atalanta has devoted her life to serving the goddess. When a group of strangers arrive to bring Atalanta to her father, she knows she must obey but doesn't want to go. It turns out that her father is a king. But what kind of king would leave his infant daughter in the woods to die? The king is ill and doesn't have much time to live. He also doesn't have a male heir. He demands that Atalanta marry and produce a grandson to rule the kingdom. But that is not in her plans. She has vowed never to marry. What will become of her?

Those Amazing Greeks!

While waiting in the supermarket checkout line, do you sometimes sneak a peek at the tabloid headlines? After all, who can resist headlines like "Garden Gnomes Found on Moon!" or "Aliens Abduct Man." Well, long before the newspapers began publishing stories like this, the Greeks did their share of entertaining people with far-out tales. How about "Three Headed Dog Guards Portal to the Underworld," or "Flying Horse Helps Hero." Do these headlines sound interesting? Then perhaps you would enjoy reading some fiction books based on Greek mythology.

As you read the Greek myths, try to identify a hook to get readers interested in the story. Create a tabloid headline to hook potential readers. Then write a paragraph to give an overview of the story as it might appear in a tabloid newspaper.

Some suggested headlines:

"Amazing Half-Boy Half-Bull Fights for Life"

"Boy Born With Feet of a Goat"

"Parents Search for Girl Abducted by Underworld Boss"

"Beautiful Women Lure Men to Their Deaths"

"Raised by Bears, Girl Becomes Great Hunter"

"Warrior Queen Kills Boyfriend"

"Man Found in Horse Returns Home"

"Girls Claim They Are Zeus' Daughters"

Greek Mythology Book List

Cooney, Caroline B. *Goddess of Yesterday*. Delacorte Press, 2002. RL 4.8, 263p
Anaxandra, daughter of the king of a small Greek island, becomes caught up in the events of the siege of Troy when, after spending most of her life as a hostage, she is taken into the palace of King Menalaus and ends up traveling to Troy as protector of Helen's infant son.

Gellis, Roberta. *Bull God*. Baen, 2000, IL or RL, 468p
A fantasy reinterpretation of the Greek myth of the Minotaur in which his half-sister, Ariadne, interpreter of the visions of Dionysus, learns that the Minotaur must either die or bring disaster upon the realm.

Hantman, Clea. *Heaven Sent*. Avon Books, 2002, RL 5.9, 172p
Polly, Era, and Thalia, banished by their father, Zeus, as punishment for a prank, accidentally end up in Athens, Georgia in 2001 where they must navigate the obstacles of a twenty-first century high school.

Hantman, Clea. *Love or Fate*. Avon Books, 2002, RL 6.3, 174p
After Thalia defies Hera's order not to use their powers, the Muses are destined to spend an eternity in Hades, unless they can outwit the furies, a three-headed dog, and Hera.

Hantman, Clea. *Muses on the Move*. Avon Books, 2002, RL 4.6, 151p
The Goddesses, a trio of Zeus' daughters who have been accidentally banished to Athens, Georgia in 2001, embark on a road trip with secret and hilarious agendas.

Hantman, Clea. *Three Girls and a God*. Avon Books, 2002, RL 6.1, 158p
Thalia's new boyfriend Dylan seems very familiar and the evil Furies are determined that the Muse sisters will not discover his true identity.

Herman, John, 1944. *Labyrinth*. Philomel Books, 2001, IL or RL, 188p
As he struggles to cope with his father's suicide and his mother's possible remarriage, 14-year-old Gregory is plagued by recurring dreams that make him question what is real.

Kindl, Patrice. *Lost in the Labyrinth: A Novel*. Houghton Mifflin, 2002, RL 6.3, 194p
Fourteen-year-old Princess Xenodice tries to prevent the death of her half-brother, the Minotaur, at the hands of the Athenian prince, Theseus, who is aided by Icarus, Daedalus, and her sister Ariadne.

Marston, Elsa. *The Ugly Goddess*. Cricket Books, 2002. IL 3-6, RL 6.5, 218p
Fourteen-year-old Princess Meret is unhappy with her future as consort of the Egyptian god Amun, especially after meeting Hector, a handsome Greek soldier. But when she is kidnapped, it is up to Hector and a young servant boy to help rescue her with the aid of the goddess Taweret.

Mason, Tom, 1958. *The Minotaur: A Novelization*. Bantam Books, 2003, 2002, RL 5.5, 137p
Alex Bellows finds himself transported to ancient Crete where he becomes Theseus, the hero who fought the bull-headed monster called the Minotaur.

McLaren, Clemence. *Aphrodite's Blessings: Love Stories from the Greek Myths*. Atheneum Books for Young Readers, 2002, IL or RL, 202p
Atalanta, Andromeda, and Psyche, three female characters in Greek mythology, tell the stories of their marriages. Includes information on love and marriage in ancient Greece.

McMullan, Kate. *Phone Home, Persephone!* Volo/Hyperion, 2002, RL 6.1, 150p
Hades, King of the Underworld, provides a corrected version of the story of how Persephone, the goddess of spring, became part-time Queen of the Underworld.

Napoli, Donna Jo, 1948. *The Great God Pan*. Wendy Lamb Books, 2003, RL 3.9, 149p
A retelling of the Greek myths about Pan, both goat and god, whose reed flute frolicking leads him to a meeting with Iphigenia, a human raised as the daughter of King Agamemnon and Queen Clytemnestra.

Napoli, Donna Jo, 1948. *Sirena*. Scholastic, 2000, 1998, IL or RL, 210p
The gods grant immortality to the mermaid Sirena when she rescues a human man from the sea and they fall in love, but his mortality creates great conflict between love and honor when he is called to defend Greece in the Trojan War.

Renault, Mary. *The King Must Die*. Vintage Books, 1988, 1986, IL or RL, 338p
Tells the story of a boy, Theseus, who must prove his manhood in a semi-barbaric society.

Spinner, Stephanie. *Quiver.* Knopf, Distributed by Random House, 2002, IL or RL, 177p
Sixteen-year-old Atalanta, abandoned as an infant, has grown to become a renowned archer and swiftest mortal alive due to the intervention of Artemis, goddess of the hunt. So when the father who forsook her so many years before issues an ultimatum that Atalanta marry and produce an heir, she counters with the condition that the man she weds must be able to best her in a footrace or die.

Yolen, Jane. *Atalanta and the Arcadian Beast.* HarperCollins, 2003, RL 5.1, 245p
Twelve-year-old Atalanta discovers a home and friendship with a bear, misunderstanding from town-dwellers, and grudging respect from the great hunter Orion, as together they pursue the mysterious creature that killed her father.

Yolen, Jane. *Hippolyta and the Curse of the Amazons.* HarperCollins, 2002, RL 5.2, 248p
Thirteen-year-old Hippolyta, a princess of the Amazons, fights to save her people from destruction when her mother the Queen refuses to sacrifice her second-born male child.

Yolen, Jane. *Odysseus in the Serpent Maze.* HarperTrophy, 2002, 2001, RL 4.7, 248p
Thirteen-year-old Odysseus, who longs to be a hero, has many opportunities to prove himself during an adventure that involves pirates and satyrs, a trip to Crete's Labyrinth, and the two young girls, Penelope and Helen, who play a major role in his future life.

Web Sites

Mythweb:
<http://www.mythweb.com/>
This site is devoted to the heroes, gods, and monsters of Greek mythology.

Greek Mythology: From the Iliad to the Fall of the Last Tyrant:
<http://www.messagenet.com/myths/>
This site includes information about the origins of the myths, a list of the names of the Immortals, fun fact quiz, and much more.

Middle Ages

Knights in shining armor. Damsels in distress. Royal banquets. All these images are part of the story of the Middle Ages. But there is a lot more to the story than these images. There is disease, war, and hard times. In these novels, we will begin to look beyond the sanitized images from the movies and see what life may have been like during that time period.

Sample Booktalk:

Avi, 1937. *Crispin: The Cross of Lead*. Hyperion Books for Children, 2002, IL 5-8, RL 5.3, 262p

Life in 1377 England is not easy for 13-year-old Asta's son. His mother has died and he is alone. He is a serf bound to Lord Furnival and has no standing in society. But something is not right. He overhears a conversation that he does not understand and the next thing he knows, he is framed for murder and declared a wolf's head. Now, he is fair game for anyone who wants to kills him for the reward money. But why? He is of no consequence--he doesn't even have a name. People all call him Asta's son. Now he learns he has a real name--Crispin. But what does that have to do with being framed for murder? As Crispin runs from the soldiers, he comes across Bear, a giant of a man who makes his living juggling and entertaining people. What will become of this unlikely pair? Will Crispin ever learn about his background and why he is in danger?

Middle Ages Book List

Avi, 1937. *Crispin: The Cross of Lead*. Hyperion Books for Children, 2002, IL 5-8, RL 5.3, 262p
Falsely accused of theft and murder, an orphaned peasant boy in fourteenth-century England flees his village and meets a larger-than-life juggler who holds a dangerous secret.

Cadnum, Michael. *The Book of the Lion*. Viking, 2000, IL YA, 204p
In 12th-century England, after his master, a maker of coins for the king, is brutally punished for alleged cheating, 17-year-old Edmund finds himself traveling to the Holy Land as squire to a knight crusader on his way to join the forces of Richard Lionheart.

Crossley-Holland, Kevin. *At the Crossing-Places*. Arthur A. Levine Books, 2002, IL 5-8, RL 5.8, 394p
Thirteen-year-old Arthur, now serving as a squire to Lord Stephen of Holt Castle, turns his attention to fulfilling some of his other dreams, such as meeting his birth mother, marrying the beautiful Winnie, and most of all, becoming a Crusader.

Crossley-Holland, Kevin. *The Seeing Stone*. Arthur A. Levine Books, 2001, IL 5-8, RL 5.9, 342p
Arthur, a thirteen-year-old boy in late 12th-century England, tells how Merlin gave him a magical seeing stone which shows him images of the legendary King Arthur, the events of whose life seem to have many parallels to his own.

Quick Flip Story

Quick Flip Story Directions:

Now that you have read a historical novel set during the time of the Middle Ages, you will create a quick flip retelling of the story.

Directions for making the book:

Use three sheets of white unlined paper. Holding them together vertically, overlap the sheets, placing one on top of the other, approximately 3/4 inch apart, from the bottom of each sheet. Hold them in that position, and fold down all three papers from the top, so they form a booklet. You should end up with a wider title page on top and five sections below. Place two staples on the fold.

Directions for book information to be included:

Label the page edges as in the picture below.

Title Page: Include the title of the book you read, the author, and your name. Draw a picture to represent the title of the book. You can use clip art if desired.

Setting: Tell where and when the story took place. Include any details to help the reader learn about the time period and setting.

Characters: Tell all about the main characters. Who they were? Are they related? Did anyone do anything interesting, special, or courageous? Draw sketches of the characters.

Problem and Solution: Choose two problems from the story and the solutions to each problem. Tell about them. Include a sketch if it helps the explanation.

Interesting Information and/orTimeline: In this section, include interesting things you learned from your book. You can draw or create a timeline of events if it is appropriate to the story you read.

Be creative! Use color, special lettering, add your own personal touches, and make this project something you are proud of! You may use cursive or print the text. You may also use the computer to word-process the text. The use of clipart is fine, too.

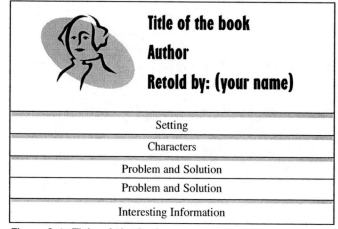

Figure 2.1: Title of the Book

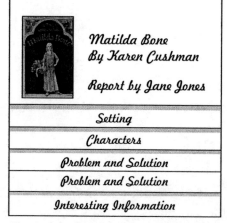

Figure 2.2: Title of the Book Example

Crowley, Bridget. *Feast of Fools*. M. K. McElderry Books, 2003, IL YA, 261p
In England in the late 13th century, a young chorister at the Cathedral of Saint Aelred, outcast because of his crippled foot, sympathizes with the city's other outcasts, the Jews, and sets out to prove their leader innocent of murder.

Cushman, Karen. *Matilda Bone*. Clarion, 2000, IL 5-8, RL 6.1, 167p
Fourteen-year-old Matilda, an apprentice bonesetter and practitioner of medicine in a village in medieval England, tries to reconcile the various aspects of her life, both spiritual and practical.

Goodman, Joan E. *Peregrine*. Houghton Mifflin, 2000, IL 5-8, RL 6.7, 222p
In 1144, fifteen-year-old Lady Edith, having lost her husband and child and anxious to avoid marrying a man she detests, sets out from her home in Surrey to go on a pilgrimage to Jerusalem.

Haahr, Berit. *The Minstrel's Tale*. Delacorte Press, 2000, IL YA, 247p
When betrothed to a repulsive old man, 13-year-old Judith runs away, assumes the identity of a young boy, and hopes to join the King's Minstrels in 14th-century England.

Love, D. Anne. *The Puppeteer's Apprentice*. M.K. McElderry Books, 2003, IL 3-6, RL 5.6, 185p
A medieval orphan girl called Mouse gains the courage she needs to follow her dreams of becoming a puppeteer's apprentice.

Malone, Patricia, 1932. *The Legend of Lady Ilena*. Dell Laurel-Leaf, 2003, 2002, IL 5-8, RL 7.3, 232p
In sixth-century Great Britain, a 15-year-old girl seeking knowledge of her lineage is drawn into battle to defend the homeland she never knew, aided by one of King Arthur's knights.

Morris, Gerald, 1963. *Parsifal's Page*. Houghton Mifflin, 2001, IL 5-8, RL 6.0, 232p
In medieval England, 11-year-old Piers' dream comes true when he becomes page to Parsifal, a peasant whose quest for knighthood reveals important secrets about both of their families.

Sauerwein, Leigh. *Song for Eloise*. Front Street, 2003, IL YA, 133p
In 12th-century France, 15-year-old Eloise, newly and unhappily married to the rough, ambitious, much older but devoted Robert of Rochefort, finds it difficult to adjust to her new life, and unwisely falls in love with the young troubadour who comes to sing at her husband's castle.

Springer, Nancy. Lionclaw: *A Tale of Rowan Hood*. Philomel Books, 2002, IL 5-8, RL 7.1, 122p
Young Lionel, minstrel in the outlaw band of Rowan Hood, daughter of Robin, tries to find his courage when she is abducted from Sherwood Forest.

Springer, Nancy. *Rowan Hood, Outlaw Girl of Sherwood Forest*. Philomel Books, 2001, IL 5-8, RL 7.1, 170p
In her quest to connect with Robin Hood, the father she has never met, 13-year-old Rosemary disguises herself as a boy, befriends a half-wolf, half-dog, a runaway princess, and an overgrown boy whose singing is hypnotic, and makes peace with her elfin heritage.

Williams, Laura E. *The Executioner's Daughter*. Henry Holt, 2000, IL 5-8, RL 7.5, 134p
Thirteen-year-old Lily, daughter of the town's executioner living in 15th-century Europe, decides whether to fight against her destiny or to rise above her fate.

Yolen, Jane. *Sword of the Rightful King: A Novel of King Arthur*. Harcourt, 2003, IL YA, 349p
Merlinnus the magician devises a way for King Arthur to prove himself the rightful king of England--pulling a sword from a stone--but trouble arises when someone else removes the sword first.

❖ Pirates ❖

A aarrgghh! Pirates. Buried treasure. Swords. Ships. There are lots of things that come to mind when we think of pirates. The life of a real pirate was much different from the fictionalized accounts we are used to reading. There have been several novels written in which we get a better idea of what a pirate's life was life. In this chapter, we'll read some books about pirates and see if we can find the clues we'll need to complete the assignment.

Sample Booktalk:

Meyer, L. A. *Bloody Jack*. Harcourt, 2002, IL 5-8, RL 6.9, 278p

Orphaned and alone at eight, Mary does what she has to do to survive. There are no orphanages to take in the children of London in the 18th century. Mary hooks up with a few other orphans and survives by begging and stealing anything else that she can. Charlie is the head of their gang and he keeps them safe; but then it happens. Charlie is killed and the gang is left with no leader. Mary begins to think about how unfair life is. It's easier being a boy. No one thinks anything about a boy being on his own. They even give you odd jobs and feed you. Right then and there, she makes a life changing decision. She cuts her hair, puts on Charlie's old clothes and becomes Jack. She signs on to a marine vessel as a ship's boy and begins her new life. The life on a ship chasing pirates is a far cry from begging on the streets of London. But how long can she get away with pretending to be a boy? She's close to 15 years old now and her body is changing and betraying her secret. Find out what life was like on a British warship searching for pirates.

Pirates Book List

Fienberg, Anna. *Horrendo's Curse*. Annick Press, Distributed in the U.S.A. by Firefly Books, 2002, IL 3-6, RL 6.2, 158p
For as long as he can remember, pirates have come to Horrendo's village to steal every 12-year-old boy. And as Horrendo approaches his 12th year he eagerly awaits his chance for adventure on the high seas.

Hausman, Gerald. *Tom Cringle: Battle on the High Seas*. Simon & Schuster Books for Young Readers, 2000, IL 3-6, RL 5.3, 185p
After Tom Cringle turns 13, he sets out on a high seas adventure that takes him to Jamaica, where he patrols the waters against pirates.

What Does It Mean?

When we think of pirates, we often think of buried treasure. To find the buried treasure, the pirates often left clues that would lead them back to the treasure. This could be a map or objects suggesting clues.

Using common objects found in the classroom, imagine how they relate to the book you have read. For instance, it you see a key, this may relate to a key to a treasure chest in the book. Write a paragraph explaining how the object relates.

Object #1
Map

Object #2
Ruler

Object #3
Door Stop

Object #4
Key

Object #5
Pen/Pencil

Jacques, Brian. *The Angel's Command: A Tale From the Castaways of the Flying Dutchman.* Philomel Books, 2003, IL 5-8, RL 8.1, 374p
Ben and Ned, a boy and dog gifted with eternal youth and the ability to communicate with one another nonverbally, encounter pirates on the high seas and rescue a kidnapped prince from a band of gypsy thieves.

Lawrence, Iain, 1955. *The Buccaneers.* Dell Yearling, 2003, 2001, IL 5-8, RL 7.4, 244p
In the 18th century 16-year-old John Spencer sails from England in his schooner, the Dragon, to the Caribbean, where he and the crew encounter pirates, fierce storms, fever, and a strange man who some fear may be cursed.

Masefield, John, 1878-1967. *Jim Davis: A High-Sea Adventure.* Scholastic, 2002, IL 3-6, RL 5.6, 224p
Jim Davis is a 12-year-old boy whose life takes a terrifying turn when he stumbles upon a ring of bloodthirsty pirates.

Meyer, L. A. (Louis A.), 1942. *Bloody Jack: Being an Account of the Curious Adventures of Mary "Jacky" Faber, Ship's Boy.* Harcourt, 2002, IL 5-8, RL 6.9, 278p
Reduced to begging and thievery in the streets of London, a 13-year-old orphan disguises herself as a boy and connives her way onto a British warship set for high sea adventure in search of pirates.

Montgomery, Hugh. *The Voyage of the Arctic Tern.* Candlewick Press, 2002, IL 5-8, RL 5.2, 212p
A simple fisherman betrays his village for a handful of jewels, a group of courageous Englishmen foils a traitorous Spanish pirate, and a lost soul seeks to redress an ancient wrong by finding a treasure chest.

Peake, Mervyn Laurence, 1911-1968. *Captain Slaughterboard Drops Anchor.* Candlewick Press, 2001, IL 3-6, RL 5.1, 47p
On a fantastic island populated by unusual animals, a pirate captain finds a trustworthy companion in the little "Yellow Creature."

Platt, Richard. *Pirate Diary: The Journal of Jake Carpenter.* Candlewick Press, 2001, IL 5-8, RL 6.2, 64p
The fictional diary of a ten-year-old boy who, in 1716, sets off from North Carolina to become a sailor, but ends up a pirate instead.

Rees, Celia. *Pirates!: The True and Remarkable Adventures of Minerva Sharpe and Nancy Kington, Female Pirates.* Bloomsbury, Distributed to the trade by Holtzbrinck, 2003, IL YA, 379p
At the dawn of the 18th century, Nancy Kington and Minerva Sharpe set sail from Jamaica on a pirate vessel, hoping to escape from an arranged marriage and slavery.

Robinet, Harriette. *the Twins, the Pirates, and the Battle of New Orleans.* Aladdin Paperbacks, 2001, 1997, IL 3-6, RL 4.8, 138p
Twelve-year-old African-American twins attempt to escape in the face of pirates, an American army, and the British forces during the Battle of New Orleans in 1815.

❖ American Revolution ❖

The study of the beginnings of our country is a staple for middle school students. It is important for students to have an understanding of where we've been before they can have a say in where we are going. In this chapter we will be reading novels that take place during that eventful time in our history.

Sample Booktalk:

Lavender, William. *Just Jane: A Daughter of England Caught in the Struggle of the American Revolution*. Harcourt, 2002, IL YA, 277p

Good day. My name is Mrs. Morley and I have been working for the Prentice family for many, many years. When Edward, the third Earl of Almsbury, passed away, it was left to me to care for his young daughter. After all, who else would do it? Edward has squandered his riches after his wife died and we had lived in humble means for the past few years. Now the Earl's young brother has agreed to take us in. Unfortunately for me, Robert is living in America. What kind of place is that for the likes of young Lady Jane? I've heard the colonies are filled with uneducated ruffians. And savages. How will we ever survive in South Carolina? The ocean passage is horrible enough but when we arrive in Charleston, Robert is nowhere to be found. He has sent his wife's brother to meet us and take us in. Robert is staying out on his plantation. I'm sure it's just some backwoods farm. But we are here and must make the most of it. To make matters worse, there is talk among some of the townsfolk about breaking with England and going their own way. Why would anyone not be loyal to England? I have heard that Robert Prentice is extremely loyal while his cousin Hugh is not. How politics can divide a family. It is just too much for me. I am here to protect Lady Jane. And I think she needs protection from more than just talk of war. It seems that several young men in the area have their sights set on her. I'm telling you. This is just too much for an old woman like me. I wish we had never left England. What will become of us in this barbaric land?

American Revolution Character

Create a character study for a character in your book. Use the gingerbread man.

Name: _____

Title of Book: _____

What did your character think about the situation?

What did your character see?

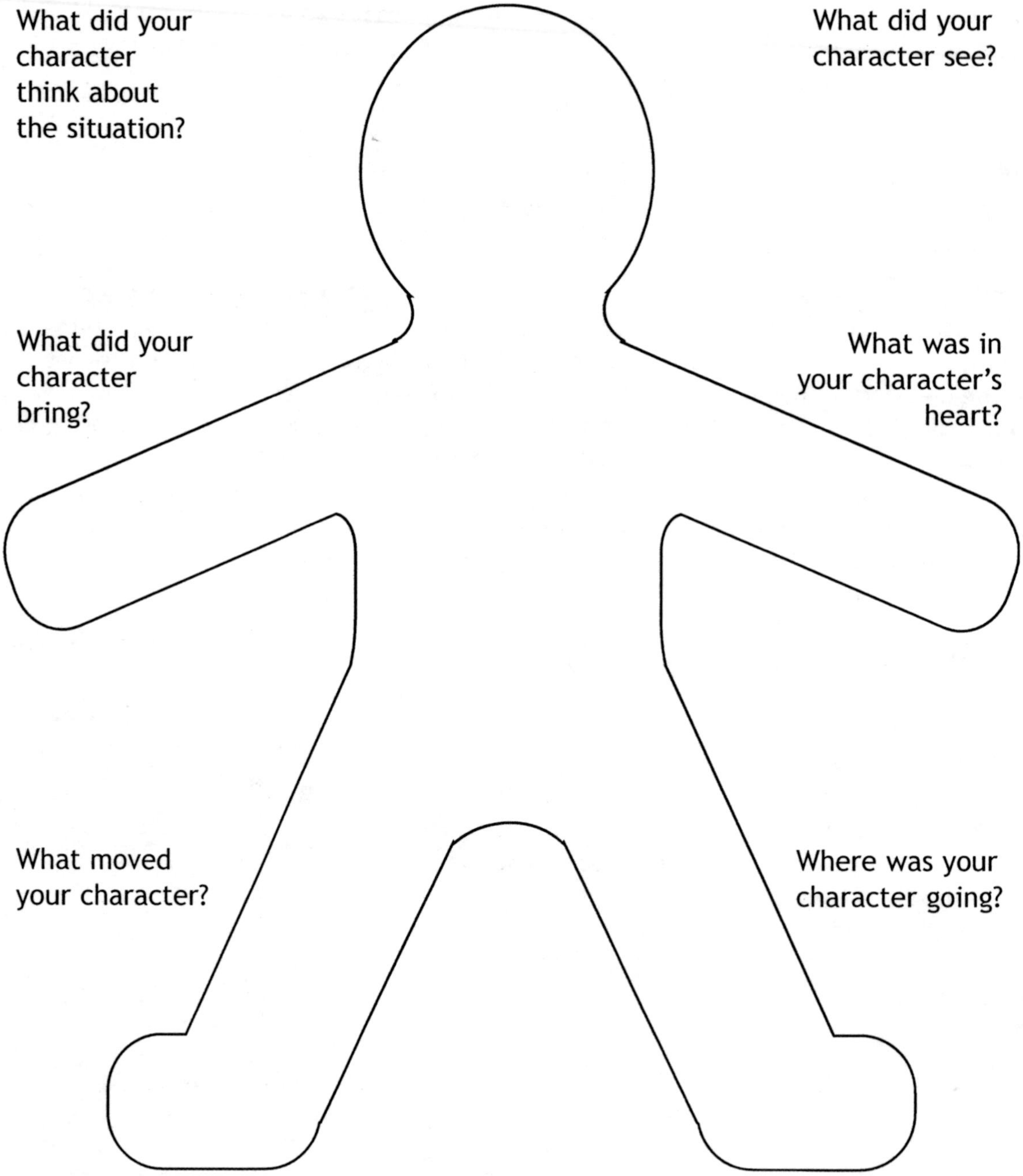

What did your character bring?

What was in your character's heart?

What moved your character?

Where was your character going?

Figure 2.3: American Revolution Character

American Revolution Book List

Borden, Louise. *Sleds on Boston Common: A Story From the American Revolution*. M. K. McElderry Books, 2000, IL 3-6, RL 5.8, 40p
Henry complains to the royal governor, General Gage, after his plan to sled down the steep hill at Boston Common is thwarted by the masses of British troops camped there.

Durrant, Lynda, 1956. *Betsy Zane: The Rose of Fort Henry*. Clarion Books, 2000, IL 5-8, RL 5.7, 198p
In 1781 twelve-year-old Elizabeth Zane, great-great-aunt of novelist Zane Grey, leaves Philadelphia to return to her brothers' homestead near Fort Henry in what is now West Virginia, where she plays an important role in the final battle of the American Revolution.

Garvie, Maureen. *George Johnson's War*. Douglas & McIntyre, Distributed in the USA by Publishers Group West, 2002, IL YA, 244p
George Johnson's comfortable life in the Mohawk Valley of New York is interrupted by the American Revolutionary War and his family sides with the Loyalists.

Guzman, Lila, 1952. *Lorenzo's Secret Mission*. Pinata Books, 2001, IL 5-8, RL 7.3, 153p
In 1776, fifteen-year-old Lorenzo Bannister leaves Texas and his father's new grave to carry a letter to the Virginia grandfather he has never known, and becomes involved with the struggle of the American Continental Army and its Spanish supporters.

Lavender, William. *Just Jane: A Daughter of England Caught in the Struggle of the American Revolution*. Harcourt, 2002, IL YA, 277p
Fourteen-year-old Jane Prentice, orphaned daughter of an English earl, arrives in Charleston, South Carolina in 1776 to find her family and her loyalties divided over the question of American independence.

Nixon, Joan Lowery. *Maria's Story, 1773*. Delacorte Press, 2001, IL 5-8, RL 7.2, 167p
In Williamsburg, Virginia two years before the start of the American Revolution, nine-year-old Maria worries that her mother will lose her contract to publish official reports and announcements of the British government because she prints anti-British articles in their family-run newspaper.

Rinaldi, Ann. *Or Give Me Death: A Novel of Patrick Henry's Family*. Harcourt, 2003, IL 5-8, RL 5.5, 226p
With their father away most of the time advocating independence for the American colonies, the children of Patrick Henry try to raise themselves, manage the family plantation, and care for their mentally ill mother.

Stephens, Amanda. *Freedom at Any Price: March 1775-April 19, 1775*. Grosset & Dunlap, 2003, IL 3-6, RL 4.9, 139p
After hearing Patrick Henry's speech and riding with Paul Revere on his famous midnight ride, the Liberty's Kids set off for Lexington, Massachusetts, where they witness the "shot heard round the world" and the start of the American Revolution.

Turner, Ann Warren. *Love Thy Neighbor: The Tory Diary of Prudence Emerson*. Scholastic, 2003, IL 5-8, RL 4.5, 188p
In Green Marsh, Massachusetts in 1774, thirteen-year-old Prudence keeps a diary of the troubles she and her family face as are Tories surrounded by American patriots at the start of the American Revolution.

❖ Civil War ❖

Less than 100 years after the birth of our country, several of the states decided to leave the union and set up an independent country. The Civil War or The War Between the States was one of the worst times in our country's history. In this chapter, students will read novels that are set during these turbulent times.

Sample Booktalk:

Peck, Richard, 1934. *The River Between Us*. Dial Books, 2003, IL YA, 164p

Howard and his father are traveling to visit Howard's grandparents in Illinois. It's an exciting trip for Howard as his father has let him help with the new Model T Ford. The year is 1916 and as Howard looks at the peeling wallpaper on the walls, he wonders how many layers would have to be peeled to find the young people that these people must have been. Grandma Tilly helps him understand when she tells him the story of the family's experience during the Civil War. Tilly's family held allegiance to the North as did most of the people in the town. But one day, an elegant young woman from New Orleans arrived and changed the family forever.

Civil War Music

During the Civil War, as with any war, many songs were written about the war. Using the web site "Music of the War Between the States" <http://home.earthlink.net/~poetry61-65/music/index.html> choose one song. Copy the lyrics of the song and then illustrate the song. There should be at least two illustrations. You may choose to illustrate each of the stanzas or create general illustrations to illustrate the mood of the entire song.

Civil War Book List

Alphin, Elaine Marie. *Ghost Soldier.* Henry Holt, 2001, IL 5-8, RL 7.6, 216p
Alexander, in North Carolina while his father decides whether to remarry and move there, meets the ghost of a Confederate soldier and helps him look for his family.

Brenaman, Miriam. *Evvy's Civil War.* G.P. Putnam, 2002, IL 5-8, RL 7.9, 209p
In Virginia in 1860, on the verge of the Civil War, 14-year-old Evvy chafes at the restrictions that her society places on both women and slaves.

Crisp, Marty. *Private Captain: A Story of Gettysburg.* Philomel Books, 2001, IL 5-8, RL 6.5, 293p
In 1863 Pennsylvania, 12-year-old Ben and his dog Captain set off in search of Ben's brother, who is missing from the Union Army.

Denslow, Sharon Phillips. *All Their Names Were Courage: A Novel of the Civil War.* Greenwillow Books, 2003, IL 3-6, RL 4.7, 135p
In 1862, as William Burd fights in the Civil War, he exchanges letters with his sister, Sallie, who is also writing to Confederate and Union generals asking about their horses in order to write a book.

Hahn, Mary Downing. *Hear the Wind Blow.* Clarion Books, 2003, IL 5-8, RL 6.9, 212p
With their mother dead and their home burned, a 13-year-old boy and his little sister set out across Virginia in search of relatives during the final days of the Civil War.

Hite, Sid. *The Journal of Rufus Rowe: A Witness to the Battle of Fredericksburg, Bowling Green*, Virginia, 1862. Scholastic, 2003, IL 5-8, RL 5.8, 132p
In 1862, sixteen-year-old Rufus Rowe runs away from home and settles in Fredericksburg, Virginia, where he documents in his journal the battle he watches unfold there.

Hughes, Pat (Patrice Raccio). *Guerrilla Season.* Farrar, Straus and Giroux, 2003, IL YA, 328p
Two 15-year-old boys in Missouri in 1863 find friendship and family loyalty tested by Quantrell's raiders, a Rebel guerrilla band who roamed under the black flag of "no quarter to be given by Union troops."

Kay, Alan N, 1965. *Nowhere to Turn.* White Mane Kids, 2002, IL 5-8, RL 5.4, 149p
In 1862, having left his uncle's farm in Pennsylvania to join the Union Army, 12-year-old Thomas experiences the bloody horror of the Battle of Antietam.

Keehn, Sally M. *Anna Sunday.* Philomel Books, 2002, IL 5-8, RL 6.0, 266p
In 1863 twelve-year-old Anna, disguised as a boy and accompanied by her younger brother Jed, leaves their Pennsylvania home and makes the difficult journey to join their wounded father in Winchester, Virginia, where they find themselves in danger from Confederate troops.

Lyons, Mary E. *Dear Ellen Bee: A Civil War Scrapbook of Two Union Spies.* Atheneum Books for Young Readers, 2000, IL 5-8, RL 5.9, 161p
A scrapbook kept by a young black girl details her experiences and those of the older white woman, "Miss Bet," who had freed her and her family, sent her north from Richmond to get an education, and then worked to bring an end to slavery. Based on the life of Elizabeth Van Lew.

Matas, Carol, 1949. *The War Within: A Novel of the Civil War.* Simon & Schuster Books for Young Readers, 2001, IL YA, 151p
In 1862, after Union forces expel Hannah's family from Holly Springs, Mississippi because they are Jews, Hannah reexamines her views regarding slavery and the war.

McMullan, Margaret. *How I Found the Strong: A Civil War Story.* Houghton Mifflin, 2004, IL 5-8, RL 6.3, 136p
Frank Russell, known as Shanks, wishes he could have gone with his father and brother to fight for Mississippi and the Confederacy, but his experiences with the war and his changing relationship with the family slave, Buck, change his thinking.

Peck, Richard, 1934. *The River Between Us.* Dial Books, 2003, IL YA, 164p
During the early days of the Civil War, the Pruitt family takes in two mysterious young ladies who have fled New Orleans to come north to Illinois.

Reeder, Carolyn. *Before the Creeks Ran Red.* HarperCollins, 2003, IL 5-8, RL 7.3, 370p
Through the eyes of three different boys, three linked novellas explore the tumultuous times beginning with the secession of South Carolina and leading up to the first major battle of the Civil War.

Rinaldi, Ann. *Numbering All the Bones.* Jump at the Sun/Hyperion Books for Children, 2002, IL 5-8, RL 6.3, 170p
Thirteen-year-old Eulinda, a house slave on a Georgia plantation in 1864, turns to Clara Barton, the eventual founder of the American Red Cross, for help in finding her brother Neddy who ran away to join the Northern war effort and is rumored to be at Andersonville Prison.

Rinaldi, Ann. *Sarah's Ground.* Simon & Schuster Books for Young Readers, 2004, IL YA, 178p
In 1861, eighteen-year-old Sarah Tracy, from New York state, comes to work at Mount Vernon, the historic Virginia home of George Washington, where she tries to protect the safety and neutrality of the site during the Civil War, and where she encounters her future husband, Upton Herbert. Includes historical notes.

Severance, John B. *Braving the Fire.* Clarion Books, 2002, IL 5-8, RL 5.7, 148p
Jem joins the Union Army but is not sure of his motives or what he hopes to accomplish, particularly since the Civil War has divided his family and caused much violence and confusion in his life.

Taylor, Mildred D. *The Land.* P. Fogelman, 2001, IL 5-8, RL 8.9, 375p
Paul-Edward, the son of a part-Indian, part-African slave mother and a white plantation owner father, finds himself caught between the two worlds of his parents as he pursues his dream of owning land in the aftermath of the Civil War.

Underground Railroad

Throughout history, the use of slaves has been a major part of the economic growth. In some parts of the United States, slavery was legal and slaves were considered property. During the second half of the 19th century, the popular view of slavery was changing and many people started viewing the practice as very wrong. Although slavery was common in the southern states, most northern states outlawed the practice. This made a trip north very enticing for slaves who wished to be free. Slaves would run away from their owners and try to make it to freedom. Organized groups of people were available to help along the way. The Underground Railroad was not a real railroad. It was a group of citizens who risked their own lives helping slaves reach freedom. The novels in this chapter deal with this period.

Sample Booktalk:

McKissack, Pat. *A Picture of Freedom: The Diary of Clotee, A Slave Girl, Belmont Plantation*, 1859. Scholastic, 1997, IL 5-8, RL 5.2, 202p

This story is told in a fictionalized diary format. Clotee is a 12-year-old slave girl living on a plantation during 1859. She has secretly learned to read and write. She must keep this a secret because slaves are forbidden to read and write. Clotee learns about the Underground Railroad that is not really a railroad but a group of people who help slaves escape from the South. Clotee is able to help others find their freedom. She must decide if she wants to leave her home and run to freedom herself.

Underground Railroad Character Study

Choose a character from your book. Answer the following questions based on your knowledge of that character.

1. **Knowledge level question:** Describe what daily life was like for your character. Write this information in the form of a paragraph.

2. **Comprehension level question:** How was your character involved in the Underground Railroad?

3. **Application level question:** If you could interview your character today, what three questions do you consider the most important and why?

4. **Analysis level question:** What was the turning point in your character's life that made him/her become involved with the Underground Railroad?

5. **Synthesis level question:** Imagine that you are a "passenger" on the Underground Railroad. Suddenly, you and the "conductor" lose your way in the dark and you have no idea where you are. What would you do? Brainstorm with your partners all the alternatives.

6. Using clay, papier-mache, paints, and construction paper, construct a map for the Underground Railroad "conductor" from South Carolina to Canada. What were the reasons you chose this particular route? What essential items must you carry with you? Why? Include this list with your map.

Underground Railroad Book List

Ayres, Katherine. *North by Night: A Story of the Underground Railroad.* Dell Yearling, 2000, 1998, IL 5-8, RL 4.8, 176p
Presents the journal of a 16-year-old girl whose family operates a stop on the Underground Railroad.

Ayres, Katherine. *Stealing South: A Story of the Underground Railroad.* Dell Yearling, 2002, 2001, IL 5-8, RL 7.5, 201p
Sixteen-year-old Will Spencer leaves home to become a peddler, but gets more than he bargained for when he agrees to go to Kentucky, steal two slaves, and help them reach their brother in Canada.

Brenaman, Miriam. *Evvy's Civil War.* G.P. Putnam, 2002, IL 5-8, RL 7.9, 209p
In Virginia in 1860, on the verge of the Civil War, 14-year-old Evvy chafes at the restrictions that her society places on both women and slaves.

Carbone, Elisa Lynn. *Stealing Freedom.* Dell Yearling, 2001, 1998, IL 5-8, RL 7.6, 258p
A novel based on the events in the life of a young slave girl from Maryland who endures all kinds of mistreatment and cruelty, including being separated from her family, but who eventually escapes to freedom in Canada.

Dahlberg, Maurine F, 1951. *The Spirit and Gilly Bucket.* Farrar, Straus and Giroux, 2002, IL 3-6, RL 6.3, 233p
In 1859, when Gilly's father goes to search for gold in the Rocky Mountains, the 11-year-old is sent to stay with her aunt and uncle in Virginia, where she befriends one of her uncle's slave girls, finds out about the Underground Railroad, and discovers that people are not always exactly as they seem.

Nordan, Robert. *The Secret Road.* Holiday House, 2001, IL 5-8, RL 5.9, 202p
Laura leaves her strict parents' Georgia plantation to spend the summer with her Quaker aunt and uncle, discovers their home is a stop on the Underground Railroad, and hatches a dangerous plan to accompany a pregnant slave to her husband and freedom.

Pearsall, Shelley. *Trouble Don't Last.* Alfred A. Knopf, Distributed by Random House, 2002, IL 5-8, RL 5.2, 237p
Samuel, an 11-year-old Kentucky slave, and Harrison, the elderly slave who helped raise him, attempt to escape to Canada via the Underground Railroad.

Pinkney, Andrea Davis. *Silent Thunder: A Civil War Story.* Jump at the Sun/Hyperion Paperbacks for Children, 2001, 1999, IL 5-8, RL 6.0, 218p
In 1862 eleven-year-old Summer and her 13-year-old brother Rosco take turns describing how life on the quiet Virginia plantation where they are slaves is affected by the Civil War.

Schotter, Roni. *F Is for Freedom.* Dorling Kindersley, 2000, IL 3-6, RL 5.5, 96p
When ten-year-old Manda interrupts a midnight delivery, she discovers her parents' involvement in the Underground Railroad and makes her own contribution to a fugitive slave's freedom.

Schwartz, Virginia Frances. *If I Just Had Two Wings.* Fitzhenry & Whiteside, 2001, IL 3-6, RL 5.8, 221p
Thirteen-year-old Phoebe uses the Underground Railroad to escape from slavery in the American South.

Woodruff, Elvira. *Dear Austin: Letters From the Underground Railroad*. Dell Yearling, 2000, 1998, IL 5-8, RL 5.3, 137p
In 1853, in letters to his older brother, 11-year-old Levi describes his adventures in the Pennsylvania countryside with his African-American friend Jupiter and his experiences with the Underground Railroad.

Wyeth, Sharon Dennis. *Flying Free*. Scholastic, 2002, IL 3-6, RL 5.4, 103p
In 1858, nine-year-old Corey Birdsong and his family, fugitive slaves from Kentucky, build a new life in Amherstburg, Canada, while still hoping to help those they left behind.

Westward Expansion

As our country outgrew its boundaries in the 1800s, many people left the settled east coast and set off to find a better life in the western part of the country. Their reasons were varied. Some left on their own accord. Some were forced. But whatever their reason, the journey was not easy. In this chapter, we will be looking at novels that describe what life may have been like for these pioneers.

 ### Sample Booktalk:

Holm, Jennifer L. *Boston Jane: An Adventure*. HarperCollins, 2001, IL 5-8, RL 8.2, 273p

Eleven-year-old Jane is somewhat of a wild child. Growing up in Philadelphia in the 1850s, Jane loved to play on the streets and toss manure at passing carriages. She also loved to help her father with his medical practice. When handsome William Brandt came to stay with them and apprentice with her father, her priorities began to change. William convinced Jane that she should strive to become a proper lady. Enrollment in Miss Hepplewhite's Young Ladies Academy pleases William but not her father. When William leaves to try his luck at the timber trade in Washington Territory, Jane wishes she can go with him. But what could a proper young lady ever do in the wilderness? When William writes to her asking her to join him and become his wife, she has to decide whether to give up her proper Philadelphia life for the uncertainty of living among the savages in the frontier. Follow Jane as she finds that you cannot learn everything in books.

Westward Expansion Projects

Projects

Reflective Journal (Verbal/Linguistic, Intrapersonal)	Using a word processor, create a reflective journal of what you may have experienced as a member of the party that traveled through the West. Be sure to include your feelings, description of the environment, the dangers, and the triumphs you experienced. Your journal must contain at least five days of entries.
PowerPoint Presentation (Visual/Spatial, Musical)	Visit the Internet site "PBS—The West" (http://www.pbs.org/weta/thewest/). Download pictures from the site. You can also use books to locate pictures and scan them into the computer. You should also find music to use in your project. Design a PowerPoint presentation that you will show as the music is played.
Square Dancing (Kinesthetic)	Music and dancing were activities frequently enjoyed by the pioneers. Research square dancing and learn one dance. Teach the dance to other students.
Singing/Teaching Songs (Musical)	Using the supplied tapes, learn to sing one of songs from the time period. Some cowboy songs can be found at <http://lonehand.com/cowboy_songs.htm> Type the lyrics on the word processor and teach the song to the class.
Oral Presentation (Naturalist, Verbal/Linguistic, Visual/Spatial)	Using the Internet or books, research the habitat of your character's destination. Prepare a short oral presentation that describes the climate, the geography, the flora, and the fauna. You may use visual aids such as weather charts, maps, and pictures.
Mock Interview (Interpersonal, Verbal/Linguistic, Visual/Spatial)	With a partner or partners, write a short skit where a newscaster travels back in time to interview a member(s) of the traveling party. You may use simple costumes and props. You may also choose to have a cameraman film your newscast. Be sure to include information in your questions and answers that would have been realistic at that time. For example, you may ask, "What made you decide to leave your home and family back East and travel to the West?"
Convince Me (Mathematical/Logical)	Take a stand on why the character should or should not have traveled West. Write 10 reasons in favor of traveling West or 10 reasons for staying behind. Think of the benefits as well as the downsides.

Westward Expansion Book List

Arrington, Frances. *Prairie Whispers*. Philomel Books, 2003, IL 5-8, RL 5.5, 184p
Only 12-year-old Colleen knows that her baby sister died just after she was born and that
Colleen put another baby in her place, until the baby's father shows up and makes trouble for
her and her family on the South Dakota prairie in the 1860s.

Cannon, A. E. (Ann Edwards). *Charlotte's Rose*. Wendy Lamb Books, 2002, IL 5-8, RL 6.7, 246p
As a 12-year-old Welsh immigrant carries a motherless baby along the Mormon Trail in 1856,
she comes to love the baby as her own and fear the day the baby's father will reclaim her.

Durbin, William, 1951. *Blackwater Ben*. Wendy Lamb Books, 2003, IL 5-8, RL 6.2, 199p
In the winter of 1898, a seventh-grade boy drops out of school to work with his father, the
cook at Blackwater Logging Camp in Minnesota.

Durbin, William, 1951. *Song of Sampo Lake*. Wendy Lamb Books, 2002, IL 5-8, RL 6.8, 217p
In 1900, as a family of Finnish immigrants begins farming on the edge of a Minnesota lake,
Matti works as a store clerk, teaches English, and works on the homestead, striving to get out
of his older brother's shadow and earn their father's respect.

Ernst, Kathleen, 1959. *Whistler in the Dark*. Pleasant Co, 2002, IL 5-8, RL 6.2, 161p
In 1868, twelve-year-old Emma and her widowed mother move to a tiny mining town in
Colorado Territory to start a newspaper, but someone is determined to scare them away.

Gregory, Kristiana. *A Journey of Faith*. Scholastic, 2003, IL 3-6, RL 5.6, 213p
Nessa leaves her orphanage in 1865 and settles in the little town of Prairie River, Kansas,
where she relies on her Christian faith to help her survive on the frontier.

Gregory, Kristiana. *Seeds of Hope: The Gold Rush Diary of Susanna Fairchild*. Scholastic, 2001,
IL 5-8, RL 6.9, 186p
A diary account of 14-year-old Susanna Fairchild's life in 1849, when her father succumbs to
gold fever on the way to establish his medical practice in Oregon after losing his wife and
money on their steamship journey from New York. Includes a historical note.

Hermes, Patricia. *A Perfect Place*. Scholastic, 2002, IL 3-6, RL 5.4, 108p
Late in 1848, nine-year-old Joshua McCullough starts a second journal, this time recording
events in Willamette Valley, Oregon Territory, as his family and others they met on the trail
begin to get settled.

Hermes, Patricia. *Westward to Home*. Scholastic, 2001, IL 3-6, RL 5.0, 108p
In 1848, nine-year-old Joshua Martin McCullough writes a journal of his family's journey from
Missouri to Oregon in a covered wagon. Includes a historical note about westward migration.

Holm, Jennifer L. *Boston Jane: An Adventure*. HarperCollins, 2001, IL 5-8, RL 8.2, 273p
Schooled in the lessons of etiquette for young ladies of 1854, Miss Jane Peck of Philadelphia
finds little use for manners during her long sea voyage to the Pacific Northwest and while
living among the American traders and Chinook Indians of Washington Territory.

Ingold, Jeanette. *Mountain Solo*. Harcourt, 2003, IL YA, 309p
Tess, a violin prodigy who has been playing since age three, throws away all her training and
talent to start a new life with her father in Montana, where she realizes having a normal life
isn't always so normal.

Kirkpatrick, Jane, 1946. *All Together in One Place: A Novel of Kinship, Courage, and Faith.* WaterBrook Press, 2000, IL YA, 406p
Young southern Wisconsin wife Mazy Bacon is perfectly content with her life until her husband decides they must head west, and the journey connects her to 11 other women in a way they never would have dreamed; based on an actual 1852 Oregon Trail incident.

Kirkpatrick, Katherine. *The Voyage of the Continental.* Holiday House, 2002, IL YA, 297p
In 1866, young orphan Emeline McCullough leaves her mill job in Lowell, Massachusetts, to head for Seattle, Washington, aboard the steamship Continental, writing in her diary about the intrigue, danger, and romance she encounters on her journey.

Levine, Ellen. *The Journal of Jedediah Barstow: An Emigrant on the Oregon Trail.* Scholastic, 2002, IL 5-8, RL 7.3, 172p
In his 1845 diary, 13-year-old orphan Jedediah describes his wagon train journey to Oregon, in which he confronts rivers and sandy plains, bears and rattlesnakes, and the challenges of living with his fellow travelers. Includes historical notes.

McCaughrean, Geraldine. *Stop The Train!: A Novel.* HarperCollins, 2003, 2001, IL 5-8, RL 6.2, 289p
Despite the opposition of the owner of the Red Rock Runner Railroad in 1893, the new settlers of Florence, Oklahoma, are determined to build a real town.

Reiss, Kathryn. *Riddle of the Prairie Bride.* Pleasant Company Publications, 2001, IL 5-8, RL 5.9, 161p
In 1878, twelve-year-old Ida Kate and her widowed father welcome a mail-order bride and her baby to their Kansas homestead, but Ida Kate soon suspects that the bride is not the woman with whom Papa has corresponded.

Seely, Debra. *Grasslands.* Holiday House, 2002, IL 3-6, RL 5.4, 170p
In the 1880s, thirteen-year-old Thomas moves west from the aristocratic Virginia home of his grandparents to a poor Kansas farm to live with a father he barely remembers and his new stepfamily.

Spooner, Michael. *Daniel's Walk.* Henry Holt, 2001, IL YA, 214p
With little more than a bedroll, a change of clothes, and a Bible, 14-year-old Daniel LeBlanc begins walking the Oregon Trail in search of his father who, according to a mysterious visitor, is in big trouble and needs his son's help.

Yep, Laurence. *When the Circus Came to Town.* HarperCollins, 2002, IL 3-6, RL 5.7, 113p
An Asian cook and a Chinese New Year celebration help a ten-year-old girl at a Montana stage coach station to regain her confidence after smallpox scars her face.

Women's Rights/Suffrage

Throughout most of history, women generally have had fewer legal rights and career opportunities than men have; being a good wife and mother was regarded as women's most significant contributions. In the 20th century, however, women in most nations won the right to vote and increased their educational and job opportunities. Perhaps most importantly, they fought for, and to a large degree accomplished, a re-evaluation of traditional views of their role in society. In this chapter, we will read novels that tell the story of the fight for women's rights.

Sample Booktalk:

Lasky, Kathryn. *A Time for Courage: The Suffragette Diary of Kathleen Bowen.* Scholastic, 2002, 2001, IL 5-8, RL 8.0, 217p

Kat is a 13 year old living in Washington DC in the year 1917. When her mother gives her a diary, she begins to write down her thoughts on school, homework, parties, and her friends. She has a pretty good life. She comes from a well-to-do family. But swirling around her is talk of politics. Particularly talk of women being allowed to vote! Kat's mother gets involved in the movement and Kat soon joins her on the picket line. What Kat finds is hostile treatment from those who oppose the women's suffrage movement. If you ever wondered about what it took for women to gain the right to vote, this is a good introduction to that time.

Women's Rights/Suffrage Book List

Cooney, Caroline B. *Prisoner of Time*. Bantam Doubleday Dell Books for Young Readers, 1999, 1998, IL YA, 200p
Attempting to break free from the oppression of women in the 19th century, 16-year-old Devonny steps through time hoping to find the power to change her fate.

Crook, Connie Brummel. *Nellie's Quest*. Stoddart Kids, 1998, IL YA, 199p
In this novel about Canadian women's rights leader Nellie McClung, set in 1895, young schoolteacher Nellie's beliefs about equality become clear as she tries to help a troubled student named Sarah and finds herself attracted to family friend, Wes.

Report to the President

Throughout most of history, women generally have had fewer legal rights and career opportunities than men have; wifehood and motherhood were regarded as women's most significant professions. In the 20th century, however, women in most nations won the right to vote and increased their educational and job opportunities. Perhaps most important, they fought for and to a large degree accomplished a re-evaluation of traditional views of their role in society.

Before you begin your exploration of the topic, brainstorm:
- What do I know about this issue?
- What are the three most important elements of this issue?
- What characteristics do the elements have in common?
- What characteristics do the elements not have in common?

In classroom groups, complete brainstorming about what you already know about events, people, situations, ideas, and concepts around women's changing rights over the time. Compare the elements and characteristics of items you brainstormed. Your group should take the Test Your Women's History I.Q. at <http://www.nwhp.org/tlp/quiz/quiz.htm>

Now that you have shared what you already know, you have a good idea of what you need to learn for this project. Look for interesting things, important things, and surprising things.
1. Choose a role (one person per role or pairs).
2. Follow your interest and what strikes you.
3. "Collect" (copy and paste) text or images from the Web to your personal digital notebook.
4. Note the location (URL) of each thing you borrow.

Questions
- How many famous women and events can I name or did I learn about in history books?
- Besides winning the right to vote in 1920, what other rights did women earn over time?
- Have women's fashions changed over time, if so why?
- How have the roles of women in work and home changed over time?
- How has the representation of women changed in different media types (i.e. movies, magazines, television shows, and software?)
- Be prepared to defend in which ways women are still discriminated against, if any.

Report to the President Continued

Roles

Historian:

The historian studies the who, what, where, when, and why.
- In what kind of documents and primary sources is the history of women kept?
- What major events mark changing roles for women overtime? Imagine you lived during a decade of the 1800-1985 time period, record a diary of 12 events of the time.
- Do we gain a better understanding of our own lives and times by understanding history?

Sociologist:

A sociologist studies the family structure, records the folklore, and profiles the people involved.
- What cultural adaptations have women made over time?
- What conflicts have caused major shifts in women's roles?
- How have women contributed to home and business environments?
- What books, magazines, poetry, and other writings have women contributed to?

Fashion designer:

The fashion designer will study clothing, hairstyles, and jewelry.
- What clothing, jewelry, and hairstyles have women worn over time?
- What trends have been recorded in clothing and other fashions?

Media tycoon:

The media tycoon will examine movies, television, radio, print media, and computer software.
- How does the role of women in past media (radio, television, advertising, movies, and software) presentations compare with that role today? Supply evidence of gender gaps in any media today.

Reports

Now you are ready to put together your report to the President on the history of women. You will be creating a PowerPoint presentation that will highlight what you have learned.

As a team, select, add, edit, and re-edit your choices of text, graphics, and sound that best inform Congress and the President that women's roles have or are changing with time. Remember to record the URLs of the sites and print sources from which you've borrowed in a Web bibliography page.

As a team, present your PowerPoint report to your classmates, and the President of the United States.

Duey, Kathleen. *Francesca Vigilucci: Washington, D.C, 1913*. Aladdin Paperbacks, 2000, IL 3-6, RL 5.7, 128p
Francesca Vigilucci is interested in the cause of the suffragists, which causes conflict with her parents.

Duffy, James, 1923. *Radical Red*. Atheneum Books for Young Readers, 1993, IL 5-8, RL 5.4, 152p
The life of a 12-year-old Irish girl living in Albany, New York, in the 1890s undergoes many changes when she and her mother become involved with Susan B. Anthony and her suffragettes.

Gaines, Ernest J, 1933. *The Autobiography of Miss Jane Pittman*. Bantam, 1972, 1971, IL YA, RL 8.0, 259p
A 110-year-old African-American woman reminisces about her life, which has stretched from the days of slavery to the black militancy and civil rights movements of the 1960s.

Hoobler, Dorothy. *The Second Decade: Voyages*. Millbrook Press, 2000, IL 3-6, RL 4.6, 159p
An Italian immigrant boy joins the large Aldrich family as they stage a women's suffrage play and listen to messages on the wireless radio about the ocean voyage of the Titanic.

Jocelyn, Marthe. *Mable Riley: A Reliable Record of Humdrum, Peril, and Romance*. Candlewick Press, 2004, IL 5-8, RL 7.4, 279p
In 1901, fourteen-year-old Mable Riley dreams of being a writer and having adventures while stuck in Perth County, Ontario, assisting her sister in teaching school and secretly becoming friends with a neighbor who holds scandalous opinions on women's rights.

Jones, Elizabeth McDavid, *1958. Secrets on 26th Street*. Pleasant Co. Publications, 1999, IL 5-8, RL 6.0, 144p
In New York City in 1914, eleven-year-old Susan encounters a mystery through an independent-minded female boarder and becomes involved in the growing suffrage movement.

Kurtz, Jane. *Bicycle Madness*. Henry Holt, 2003, IL 3-6, RL 3.7, 122p
In the late 19th century, Lillie gains friendship and help with a spelling bee from a neighbor, Frances Willard, who braves criticism to speak about women's rights and learn to ride a bicycle. Includes historical notes.

Lasky, Kathryn. *A Time for Courage: The Suffragette Diary of Kathleen Bowen*. Scholastic, 2002, 2001, IL 5-8, RL 8.0, 217p
A diary account of 13-year-old Kathleen Bowen's life in Washington, D.C. in 1917, as she juggles concerns about the national battle for women's suffrage, the war in Europe, and her own school work and family. Includes a historical note.

Oneal, Zibby. *A Long Way to Go*. Puffin Books, 1992, 1990, IL 3-6, RL 4.8, 54p
Eight-year-old Lila deals with the women's suffrage movement that rages during World War I.

⚜ Great Depression ⚜

During the fall of 1929, an event happened that changed the lives of all Americans. The Stock Market crashed. Added to other events during the time, this brought about the time known as the Great Depression. People lost their jobs, their savings, their homes, and their hope for the future. Desperate measures were needed to bring the country out of the depth of the economic problems. In this chapter, we will read novels that take place during the Great Depression and then study the policies of Roosevelt's New Deal that helped the country endure.

Sample Booktalk:

Moss, Marissa. *Rose's Journal: The Story of a Girl in the Great Depression*. Harcourt, 2003, IL 3-6, RL 5.0, 52p

Rose lives in Kansas and the year is 1935. It's during a period of time known as the Great Depression. Many people were out of work. The farmers were suffering too. There was a drought that lasted for several years. Because of the lack of rain, the land dried up and the farmers were unable to grow crops. Many lost their farms when they couldn't pay their bills. Rose's family wants to keep their farm but things are not looking good. The soil is so dry that dust is blown all around. Some days it gets so bad that they can't even see where they are going. Even though they want to stay, things are getting so bad that Rose's family may be forced to leave the farm just like many of their neighbors.

Great Depression Book List

Austin, Lynn N. *Hidden Places: A Novel*. Bethany House, 2001, IL or RL, 429p
Young widow Eliza, left alone to run Wyatt Orchards and raise three children, does not know how she is going to manage, when a stranger, Gabe, appears at her doorstep and turns out to be the answer to her prayers.

Curtis, Christopher Paul. *Bud, Not Buddy*. Delacorte Press, 1999, RL 5.6, 245p
Ten-year-old Bud, a motherless boy living in Flint, Michigan, during the Great Depression, escapes a bad foster home and sets out in search of the man he believes to be his father--the renowned bandleader, H.E. Calloway of Grand Rapids.

Earley, Tony, 1961. *Jim the Boy: A Novel*. Little, Brown and Co, 2000, IL or RL, 227p
Jim, living with his mother and three uncles in the small hamlet of Aliceville, North Carolina, comes of age in the Depression years and begins to realize the largeness of the world outside his happy home.

Garlock, Dorothy. *With Hope*. Warner Books, 1998, IL or RL, 464p
Henry Ann, left to raise her two rebellious half-siblings in the middle of Oklahoma's dust bowl in 1932, finds a ray of hope when new neighbor Tom Dolan moves in. But she soon discovers Tom has problems of his own, and the two must stand together if their love is to survive.

New Deal News

After reading about the Great Depression, students will then find how the government responded to the times. Students will identify and describe the various programs and agencies developed by President Roosevelt as part of the New Deal economic policy. They will also be able to explain how these programs still affect us today.

Students will individually research the variety of programs and agencies created through New Deal legislation and then work in groups to create articles for a newspaper that will demonstrate their understanding of the New Deal program and its continued impact. The articles will need to include at least two programs associated with relief, recovery, and reform. In addition, students will need to include at least one article that shows how the New Deal still affects us today. To do this, they may summarize an existing current event article (e.g., Social Security reform) or create an original article (e.g., FDIC insuring bank deposits).

In cooperative learning groups, students will construct knowledge as they write articles and provide appropriate illustrations and photographs for their newspaper. In this portion of the unit, the teacher will take on the role of a facilitator and help students work with facts and details while helping them to improve the quality of their work.

Lastly, each group will present their newspaper to the class, highlighting how they met the rubric's content and communication requirements.

Haseley, Dennis. *The Amazing Thinking Machine*. Dial Books, 2002, RL 5.8, 117p
During the Great Depression, while their father is away looking for work, eight-year-old Patrick and 13-year-old Roy create a machine to help their mother make ends meet, even as she is helping tramps.

Janke, Katelan. *Survival in the Storm: The Dust Bowl Diary of Grace Edwards*. Scholastic, 2002, RL 6.8, 189p
A 12-year-old girl keeps a journal of her family's and friends' difficult experiences in the Texas panhandle, part of the "Dust Bowl," during the Great Depression. Includes a historical note about life in America in 1935.

Moss, Marissa. *Rose's Journal: The Story of a Girl in the Great Depression*. Harcourt, 2003, IL 3-6, RL 5.0, 52p
Rose keeps a journal of her family's difficult times on their farm during the days of the Dust Bowl in 1935.

Peck, Richard, 1934. *A Long Way From Chicago: A Novel in Stories*. Dial Books for Young Readers, 1998, RL 4.2, 148p
A boy recounts his annual summer trips to rural Illinois with his sister during the Great Depression to visit their larger-than-life grandmother.

Porter, Tracey. *Treasures in the Dust*. HarperTrophy, 1999, RL 5.5, 148p
Eleven-year-old Annie and her friend Violet tell of the hardships endured by their families when dust storms, drought, and the Great Depression hit rural Oklahoma.

Ryan, Pam Munoz. *Esperanza Rising*. Scholastic, 2000, RL 6.2, 262p
Esperanza and her mother are forced to leave their life of wealth and privilege in Mexico to go work in the labor camps of Southern California, where they must adapt to the harsh circumstances facing Mexican farm workers on the eve of the Great Depression.

Whitmore, Arvella. *The Bread Winner*. Houghton Mifflin, 1990, RL 5.2, 138p
When both her parents are unable to find work and pay the bills during the Great Depression, resourceful Sarah Ann Puckett saves the family from the poorhouse by selling her prize-winning homemade bread.

Web Sites

New Deal Network:
<http://newdeal.feri.org/>
Annotation missing

American Memory Project:
<http://memory.loc.gov/ammem/fsowhome.html>
Annotation missing

❖ Holocaust ❖

During World War II, the Nazis executed millions of Jews because of their religion. It is important for us to remember this time and the devastation it caused so that we can ensure it will never happen again. Many of those who entered the concentration camps did not survive to tell their stories. But enough survived to tell of the horror that took so many valuable lives. In this chapter, we will read novels that tell of the times during the Holocaust.

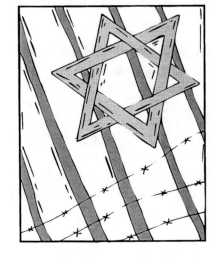

Sample Booktalk:

Spinelli, Jerry. *Milkweed*. Thorndike Press, 2004, 2003, IL YA, 282p

He's a young boy with nothing to lose. Not even a name. He's called Stop Thief, runt, fast. He's just living day to day until he meets Uri. Uri is an orphan who takes the young boy under his wing and gives him a name and a made up history. He is now Misha and he steals to feed himself and his new friends. Life is certainly not easy in Warsaw during the Nazi occupation, and certainly not if you are a Jew. Misha knows nothing of politics or war or oppression so he doesn't know to be afraid of the Jackboots. He has nothing to lose and no way of knowing what life has to offer beyond his own point of reference.

Holocaust Book List

Belliveau, G. K. (Gregory Kenneth), 1965. *Go Down to Silence: A Novel*. Multnomah Publishers, 2001, IL YA, 343p
Jacob Horowitz visits a friend, a former member of the Belgian underground, and together, the two men share the experiences they had during the Holocaust with Jacob's estranged son.

Bennett, Cherie. *Anne Frank and Me*. Putnam's, 2001, IL YA, 291p
After suffering a concussion while on a class trip to a Holocaust exhibit, Nicole finds herself living the life of a Jewish teenager in Paris during the Nazi occupation.

Denenberg, Barry. *One Eye Laughing, the Other Weeping: The Diary of Julie Weiss*. Scholastic, 2000, IL 5-8, RL 6.3, 250p
During the Nazi persecution of the Jews in Austria, 12-year-old Julie escapes to America to live with her relatives in New York City.

Isaacs, Anne. *Torn Thread*. Scholastic Press, 2000, IL 5-8, RL 6.8, 188p
In an attempt to save his daughter's life, Eva's father sends her from Poland to a labor camp in Czechoslovakia where she and her sister survive the war.

Holocaust Investigation

The books in this section will give an introduction to keywords such as WWII, rescuers, resistance, Denmark, Jews, and heroes.

Students should choose one of the following Web sites to investigate further. Students should take notes and relate the information found on the Web site with the book they have read. Make sure they include the URL on their note cards

■ <http://www.ushmm.org/education>: The Holocaust Museum
Tour the Holocaust Museum at this site. There is information for students as well as teachers. The links to people and their stories make it very personal.

■ <http://www.homeofheroes.com/>: "I Am an American"
When the Pacific theater of WWII began, Nisei, second generation Japanese Americans, became an issue. They were declared 4-F (unfit for service) of 4-C (enemy aliens). Eventually they were allowed to serve in their own battalion. This site will be an eye opening experience for the students after knowing how the Jews were "relocated." There is a section of the site called Hall of Heroes Museum, which leads to a Special Hall of Heroes Feature. When clicking on "Go for Broke," the story of the treatment of Japanese Americans by our government can be equated to the Jews. Their determination to serve made them heroes.

■ <http://www.jewishsf.com/bk951020/sfadane.htm>: "Danish Rescuer of Jews Tells Story of Simple Humanity"
Preben Munch-Nielsen, a member of the Resistance Movement in his youth, tells his part in freeing the Jews. This site is a bulletin to notify people of Preben Munch-Nielsen's speaking engagements, but his story supports the details they read in novels. An interview with a person who has rescued the Jews makes the information they've read personal, rather than a fictional character from a book. The town he was from helps to support the idea that more than one town in Denmark participated in this venture.

■ <http://www.ushmm.org/outreach/denmark.htm>: "Rescue in Denmark"
This site gives information on the hiding places, underground escape routes, false papers, etc. as tactics rescuers used. This site also refers to things other than hiding places that were provided by the rescuers. Reference to the underground can help the class connect with the Underground Railroad of the Civil War. The statistics for the number of Jews saved and taken to camps reflects on the Danish and their concern for their fellow citizens. The article makes reference to other countries trying to help in the rescue.

Holocaust Investigation Continued

- <http://www.humboldt.edu/~rescuers/index.html>: "To save one life is as if you have saved the world"
This site has many biography entries about people who went out of their way to save the Jews.

- <http://www.humboldt.edu/~rescuers/book/album/album.html>: "Album of Rescuers"
This album has shortened reviews and pictures of rescuers. There are some interesting stories that depict different ways some people managed to help rescue the Jews other than putting them on boats or hiding them.

- <http://www.yad-vashem.org.il/righteous/index_righteous.html>: "The Righteous Among the Nations"
"The Righteous Among the Nations" is an award to recognize rescuers who helped during WWII. Yad Vashem, located in Jerusalem, Israel is a museum and exhibit halls commemorating the people who helped the Jews. The site recognizes particular people and how they helped the cause.

- <http://tqjunior.thinkquest.org/4616/index.html>: "World War II: An American Scrapbook"
This site has stories written by children who have grandparents and great grandparents who served in WWII. The children feel their relatives are heroes. Since this site is written by children and for children, it puts the language at their level. The authors of the stories tell how these interviews have made WWII come alive, rather than just something from history. Readers are encouraged to talk to their families about WWII experiences.

- <http://www.almondseed.com/vfry/>: "Varian Fry, The forgotten hero who displayed extraordinary courage. . ."
This site tells the story of a New York City man who went to France on a mission, which helped save persons who turned out to be prominent writers, sculptors, and artists.

Johnston, Tony, 1942. *The Harmonica*. Charlesbridge, 2004, IL 3-6, RL 6.3, 32p
Torn from his home and parents in Poland during World War II, a young Jewish boy, starving in a concentration camp, finds hope in playing Schubert on his harmonica, even when the commandant orders him to play.

Kacer, Kathy. *Clara's War*. Second Story Press, 2001, IL YA, 189p
After young Clara and her family are sent by the Nazis to the Czechoslovakian ghetto of Terezin, she copes by looking forward to auditions for a children's opera, "Brundibar"--but plans change when she learns her friend Jacob is plotting an escape.

Kacer, Kathy. *The Night Spies*. Second Story Press, 2003, IL 5-8, RL 7.4, 197p
Presents a fact-based story in which Gabi and her young cousin Max, hiding in a hayloft to avoid detection by the Nazis during World War II, begin taking late-night excursions into the nearby woods and come across information that leads to their involvement with the anti-Nazi partisan soldiers.

Levitin, Sonia, 1934. *Room in the Heart*. Dutton, 2003, IL YA, 290p
After German forces occupy Denmark during World War II, 15-year-old Julie Weinstein and 15-year-old Niels Nelson and their friends and families try to cope with their daily lives, finding various ways to resist the Nazis and, ultimately, to survive.

Mercati, Cynthia. *The Secret Room*. Perfection Learning, 2000, IL 5-8, RL 3.9, 72p
Two girls who are friends become separated in Nazi-occupied Europe during World War II.

Newbery, Linda. *Sisterland*. *David Fickling Books*, 2004, 2003, IL YA, 369p
When Hilly's grandmother becomes ill with Alzheimer's disease, her family is turned upside down by revelations from her life during World War II.

Orlev, Uri, 1931. *Run, Boy, Run: A Novel*. Houghton Mifflin, 2003, IL YA, 186p
Based on the true story of a nine-year-old boy who escapes the Warsaw Ghetto and must survive throughout the war in the Nazi-occupied Polish countryside.

Patz, Nancy. *Who Was The Woman Who Wore The Hat?* Dutton Books, 2003, IL 3-6, RL 3.2, 40p
The author, having seen an unlabeled, solitary women's hat displayed in Amsterdam's Jewish Historical Museum, ponders the joys and sufferings its unknown owner might have experienced.

Pressler, Mirjam. *Malka*. Philomel Books, 2003, IL YA, 280p
In the winter of 1943, a Polish physician and her older daughter make a dangerous and arduous trek to Hungary while seven-year-old Malka, who they were forced to leave behind when she became ill, fends for herself in a ghetto.

Ross, Stewart. *The Star Houses: A Story From the Holocaust*. Barron's, 2002, IL 5-8, RL 8.9, 86p
Teenager Bandi Guttmann, a Hungarian Jew, is forced to move with his family into a "star house" as the Nazis' grip on his country grows tighter. Based on a true story.

Schmidt, Gary D. *Mara's Stories: Glimmers in the Darkness*. Henry Holt, 2001, IL 5-8, RL 5.9, 149p
Each evening, in one of the barracks of a Nazi death camp, a woman shares stories that push back the darkness, cold, and fear, bringing hope to the women and children who listen.

Spinelli, Jerry. *Milkweed*. Thorndike Press, 2004, 2003, IL YA, 282p
A street child, known to himself only as Stopthief, finds community when he is taken in by a band of orphans in a Warsaw ghetto, which helps him weather the horrors of the Nazi regime.

Wiseman, Eva, 1947. *My Canary Yellow Star*. Tundra Books of Northern New York, 2002, 2001, IL 3-6, RL 5.9, 232p
A novel about a young Jewish girl in Budapest who suffers worse and worse conditions under Nazi rule until hope arrives in the form of a foreign man who risks his own life to save others. Based on the real-life efforts of Raoul Wallenberg, a Swedish diplomat who saved up to 100,000 lives during the Second World War.

Life on the Home Front

During World War II, the United States was fighting in a major war that took many men away from their normal lives. Family, friends, and careers were left behind when they left to fight in the war. Although no major battle was fought on United States soil, the people on the home front were very much involved in the war. Civilians supported the war efforts either directly or indirectly. In this chapter, we will be reading novels set during this time that illustrate what life was like on the home front.

Sample Booktalk:

Kochenderfer, Lee. *The Victory Garden*. Delacorte Press, 2002, IL 3-6, RL 5.9, 167p

Theresa's life has been a lot different since her brother went into the military to fight in World War II. Many things on the home front are different. There are shortages of just about everything. In school, paper is scarce and children use what they can to do their assignments. Clothes are patched and reworked--never just thrown away. Theresa's father's bootery is doing well since people can only resole their shoes, not buy new ones. And now food is being rationed as well. All over the country, people are starting to plant their own vegetable gardens to supplement what food is available. These gardens are encouraged so that farmers can send their vegetables to other places in the world in hopes of ending the war sooner. The Victory Gardens are important in many other ways as well. Find out what happens when a group of children help a neighbor in *The Victory Garden*.

Life on the Home Front

Complete the activities based on your independent reading book.

READING	RESEARCH	SKILLS	CREATIVE OPTIONS
Pair with someone who has read a different book. Create a Venn diagram comparing the two stories	Research conscientious objectors. How did they play a role in the war effort?	You are a teenager living during the war. Write a letter to a soldier fighting the war telling him how you feel about his role.	People had to do without many of the items they were used to. Create a poster encouraging rationing.
Read about an event that happened during the time period. Write four journal entries about the event from the point of view of someone involved.	Research Franklin Roosevelt's speech on the declaration of war. Write a one-page report on the reaction to the speech.	Create a timeline of events that led to World War II and the United States' involvement.	Many people back home kept track of the fighting by making maps. Use a map of Europe and track troop movements.
Find a nonfiction book about life on the home front. Write at least five note cards. Each note card will have "Main Idea" at the top and 3-5 details below.	The people at home eagerly looked for useful things to do and found them. Research and report on some of the civilian jobs that supported the war effort.	Write a journal from the perspective of a child whose father is fighting overseas. Be sure to include activities the child is involved in as well as thoughts and fears.	You are applying for the job of air raid warden for your town. Write a statement outlining your qualifications for the job.
Find song lyrics or poems about the time period or write your own that is at least three stanzas. Read or recite it to the class.	Research the role women played on the home front. Come prepared to report to the class. You may dress in character.	Write a radio script telling about some aspect of life on the home front.	Create a mural that tells the story from your book. Write facts that you learned and draw a picture to illustrate them.

Grading rubric:

A = Complete at least 8 well-done projects.
B = Complete at least 6 projects with at least one in each column.
C = Complete at least 4 projects from each column. The projects must be well done to receive a C.
Poor work will be given the grade of D or F.

Life on the Home Front Book List

Copeland, Cynthia L. *Elin's Island*. Millbrook Press, 2003, IL 5-8, RL 7.4, 144p
Thirteen-year-old Elin can't imagine living anywhere but the island off the coast of Maine where her father is lightkeeper, until the night in 1941 when she awakes to the sound of German torpedoes while her parents are on the mainland.

Davies, Jacqueline. *Where the Ground Meets the Sky*. M. Cavendish, 2002, IL 3-6, RL 4.2, 224p
During World War II, a 12-year-old girl is uprooted from her quiet, East coast life and moved to a secluded army post in the New Mexico desert where her father and other scientists are working on a top secret project.

Denenberg, Barry. *The Journal of Ben Uchida, Citizen 13559: Mirror Lake Internment Camp*. Scholastic, 1999, IL 5-8, RL 6.2, 156p
Twelve-year-old Ben Uchida keeps a journal of his experiences as a prisoner in a Japanese internment camp in Mirror Lake, California, during World War II.

Gaeddert, LouAnn Bigge. *Friends and Enemies*. Atheneum Books for Young Readers, 2000, IL 5-8, RL 6.4, 177p
In 1941 in Kansas, as America enters World War II, 14-year-old William finds himself alienated from his friend Jim, a Mennonite who does not believe in fighting for any reason, as they argue about the war.

Giff, Patricia Reilly. *Lily's Crossing*. Delacorte, 1997, IL 3-6, RL 5.2, 180p
During a summer spent at Rockaway Beach in 1944, Lily's friendship with a young Hungarian refugee causes her to see the war and her own world differently.

Harlow, Joan Hiatt. *Shadows on the Sea*. M.K. McElderry Books, 2003, IL 5-8, RL 6.6, 244p
In 1942, fourteen-year-old Jill goes to stay with her grandmother on the coast of Maine, where she is introduced to the often gossipy nature of small-town life, and discovers that the war is closer than she thought.

Kerr, M. E. *Slap Your Sides: A Novel*. HarperCollins, 2001, IL YA, 198p
Life in their Pennsylvania hometown changes for Jubal Shoemaker and his family when his older brother witnesses to his Quaker beliefs by becoming a conscientious objector during World War II.

Kochenderfer, Lee. *The Victory Garden*. Delacorte Press, 2002, IL 3-6, RL 5.9, 167p
Hoping to contribute to the war effort during World War II, eleven-year-old Teresa organizes her friends to care for an ill neighbor's victory garden.

Lisle, Janet Taylor. *The Art of Keeping Cool*. Atheneum Books for Young Readers, 2000, IL 5-8, RL 6.2, 207p
In 1942, Robert and his cousin Elliot uncover long-hidden family secrets while staying in their grandparents' Rhode Island town, where they also become involved with a German artist who is suspected of being a spy.

Mazer, Norma Fox, 1931. *Good Night, Maman*. HarperTrophy, 2001, 1999, IL 5-8, RL 5.0, 185p
After spending years fleeing from the Nazis in war-torn Europe, 12-year-old Karin Levi and her older brother Marc find a new home in a refugee camp in Oswego, New York.

Myers, Anna. *Captain's Command*. Walker, 1999, IL 5-8, RL 5.0, 134p
Even as Christmas approaches and Gail longs to hear that her soldier father has not been killed in World War II, the sixth grader helps bring her handicapped uncle back to life.

Osborne, Mary Pope. *My Secret War: The World War II Diary of Madeline Beck*. Scholastic, 2000, IL 5-8, RL 5.5, 186p
Thirteen-year-old Madeline's diaries for 1941 and 1942 reveal her experiences living on Long Island during World War II while her father is away in the Navy.

Reeder, Carolyn. *Foster's War*. Scholastic, 2000, 1998, IL 5-8, RL 7.5, 267p
When his older brother joins the army during World War II in order to escape the rages of an authoritarian father, 11-year-old Foster fights his battles on the homefront.

Twomey, Cathleen. *Beachmont Letters*. Boyds Mills Press, 2003, IL YA, 223p
Scarred by a fire that killed her father, a 17-year-old girl begins a correspondence with a young soldier in 1944.

Ylvisaker, Anne. *Dear Papa*. Candlewick Press, 2002, IL 5-8, RL 5.4, 184p
In September of 1943, one year after her father's death, nine-year-old Isabelle begins writing him letters, which are interspersed with letters to other members of her family, relating important events in her life and how she feels about them.

Zindel, Paul. *The Gadget*. HarperCollins, 2001, IL 5-8, RL 5.8, 184p
In 1945, having joined his father at Los Alamos, where he and other scientists are working on a secret project to end World War II, thirteen-year-old Stephen becomes caught in a web of secrecy and intrigue.

Civil Rights Movement

During the middle of the 20th century, the civil rights movement made headlines behind the leadership of Martin Luther King, Jr. Dr. King believed in peaceful protest and led massive demonstrations demanding equal rights for African Americans. The peaceful demonstrations sometimes gave way to violent interactions. In this chapter, students will be reading novels about the time period and the people who lived it.

Sample Booktalk:

Rodman, Mary Ann. *Yankee Girl*. Farrar, Straus and Giroux, 2004, IL 5-8, RL 6.3, 219p

The year is 1964. Alice and her family have just moved into their new home in Mississippi. Alice didn't want to leave Chicago but her father's job with the FBI caused them to move every couple of years. Alice felt that this would be like the other moves. She would make some friends and then move to another place leaving them behind. What she couldn't know is that this would not be like the other moves at all. Right from the start she found out that the kids here did not want to be friends with a Yankee from Chicago. A Yankee who couldn't understand their ways. To top it all off, the school was being forced to integrate and now "negras" would be side by side with the whites. When Alice tries to befriend the new girl, she learns a lesson she would rather not know. That there was no way for a Negro girl and a white girl in Mississippi to be friends. No way. Not in 1964.

Civil Rights Book List

Armistead, John. *The Return of Gabriel*. Milkweed Editions, 2002, IL 5-8, RL 5.6, 218p
In the summer of 1964, a 13-year-old white boy whose best friend is black is caught in the middle when civil rights workers and Ku Klux Klan members clash in a small town near Tupelo, Mississippi.

Collier, Kristi. *Jericho Walls*. Henry Holt, 2002, IL 5-8, RL 5.8, 213p
In 1957, when her preacher father accepts a post in Jericho, Alabama, Jo wants to fit in, but her growing friendship with an African-American boy forces her to confront the racism of the South and to reconsider her own values.

Curtis, Christopher Paul. *The Watsons Go to Birmingham-1963: A Novel*. Delacorte Press, 1995, IL 5-8, RL 5.0, 210p
The ordinary interactions and everyday routines of the Watsons, an African-American family living in Flint, Michigan, are drastically changed after they go to visit Grandma in Alabama in the summer of 1963.

Civil Rights Movement Final Activity "Reader's Theater"

Task:

You will perform a scene from the book you chose to read for this unit. You may perform the scene alone or with others who read the same book.

Guidelines:

- Choose a favorite scene from the book you read.

- Individually or with a small group, write a script. You may use dialogue taken directly from the text or may paraphrase as long as you stay true to the text.

- You do not have to memorize the script. Each group member is responsible for having his or her own script to read from.

- One copy of the script, with names of all performers listed, must be turned in to the teacher before the start of your performance.

- Be creative. For instance, try speaking using the dialect or accent that the characters may have used. Females may portray males and vice versa.

- Props and costumes are not necessary, but will certainly add to your performance. The script and how you perform it are more important than what you are wearing!

- Practice, practice, practice!! Be prepared to perform a five-minute play for your class.

- Have fun! You worked hard on this unit and now is your chance to share your favorite book with the rest of the class.

Davis, Ossie. *Just Like Martin*. Puffin Books, 1995, IL 5-8, RL 5.9, 215p
Following the deaths of two classmates in a bomb explosion at his Alabama church, 14-year-old Stone organizes a children's march for civil rights in the autumn of 1963.

Gaines, Ernest J, 1933. *The Autobiography of Miss Jane Pittman*. Bantam, 1972, 1971, IL YA, RL 8.0, 259p
A 110-year-old African-American woman reminisces about her life, which has stretched from the days of slavery to the black militancy and civil rights movements of the 1960s.

Herschler, Mildred Barger. *The Darkest Corner*. Front Street, 2000, IL 5-8, RL 5.4, 240p
Her loving relationship with the black woman who works for her family and her friendship with two black neighbors in the small Mississippi town where she grows up in the 1950s and 1960s brings Teddy into conflict with her racist father, a member of the local Ku Klux Klan.

McGuigan, Mary Ann. *Where You Belong: A Novel*. Atheneum Books for Young Readers, 1997, IL 5-8, RL 7.5, 171p
In 1963, when 13-year-old Fiona runs away from home and ends up reunited with her former classmate Yolanda in an all-black neighborhood of the Bronx, their interracial friendship gives rise to both comfort and controversy.

Murphy, Rita. *Black Angels*. Dell Yearling, 2002, 2001, IL 3-6, RL 5.0, 163p
The summer of 1961 brings change to 11-year-old Celli and her town of Mystic, Georgia, when her beloved Sophie becomes involved in the Civil Rights Movement and Celli learns a secret about the father who left her and her family long ago.

Nelson, Vaunda Micheaux. *Beyond Mayfield*. G.P. Putnam's, 1999, IL 5-8, RL 6.3, 138p
In 1961 the children of Mayfield are concerned with air-raid drills and fallout shelters, but the civil rights movement becomes real when a neighbor joins the Freedom Riders.

Robinet, Harriette. *Walking to the Bus-Rider Blues*. Atheneum Books for Young Readers, 2000, IL 3-6, RL 4.9, 146p
Twelve-year-old Alfa Merryfield, his older sister, and their grandmother struggle for rent money, food, and their dignity as they participate in the Montgomery, Alabama bus boycott in the summer of 1956.

Rodman, Mary Ann. *Yankee Girl*. Farrar, Straus and Giroux, 2004, IL 5-8, RL 6.3, 219p
When her FBI-agent father is transferred to Jackson, Mississippi, in 1964, eleven-year-old Alice wants to be popular but also wants to reach out to the one black girl in her class in a newly-integrated school.

Modern Day Refugees

It is hard to imagine what it is like to be a refugee. You must leave everything you know behind and begin a completely new life. Often, refugees are forced to leave with little advanced warning and little time to pack up their belongings. Refugees are not generally able to make a plan as to where to go or what to bring with them. This leaves them ill-prepared to face what is thrown at them in the future.

 ## Sample Booktalk:

Mikaelsen, Ben, 1952. *Red Midnight*. HarperTrophy/Rayo, 2003, 2002, RL 4.1, 212p

Santiago's father once told him that changes do not always ask our permission. Little did Santiago know how true that would become in his life. When the soldiers came to his town in Guatemala that night, men, women, and children were killed and the village was burned. Twelve-year-old Santiago and his four-year-old sister Angelina escape the soldiers terror. Now, there is only one hope for the two children. They must travel to their Uncle's home. It is not an easy journey and it may take several days. When they reach their Uncle's home, they will begin the next part of their journey. They have made a promise to escape to the United States and tell the people about the butchery of the Guatemalan soldiers. But is it even possible? They have only a small sea kayak and a big ocean between them and freedom. There are also soldiers, pirates, and sharks. Not to mention storms. How can two small children with no sailing experience ever hope to find freedom? Join Santiago and Angelina as they journey towards the unknown.

"It's Time to Go—Pack Your Bags"

In this activity, students will imagine themselves in the position of a forced migrant. They will be given two minutes to gather their belongings. They have free reign to choose what to bring. They are to imagine leaving their home and their community and will not be able to return. Students can work in groups to brainstorm what items should be packed.

After students decide on their choices, have them discuss the items and give an explanation of why the items were chosen and how they will help the refugee. Some questions to further the discussion should include:

- What did you take with you? Why?

- Why did you think you would need these things?

- Did you take identification/documentation with you? Why would you need this? If you did not bring this, how can you prove who you are?

After the discussion, have students work together to revise their lists. What did they change and why?

Modern Day Refugees Book List

Bernardo, Anilu. *Jumping Off to Freedom*. Pinata Books, 1996, IL or RL, 198p
Courage and desperation lead 15-year-old David and his father to flee Cuba's repressive regime and seek freedom by taking to the sea on a raft headed for Miami.

Buss, Fran Leeper, 1942. *Journey of the Sparrows*. Puffin, 2002, RL 6.3, 155p
Maria and her brother and sister, Salvadoran refugees, are smuggled into the United States in crates and try to eke out a living in Chicago with the help of a sympathetic family.

Choyce, Lesley, 1951. *Refuge Cove*. Orca Book, 2002, IL or RL, 89p
Greg, having just moved to Deep Cove with his mother following the sudden death of his dad, finds friends and a new purpose in life when he rescues a family of refugees who have come to Canada from Asia.

Ellis, Deborah, 1960. *Mud City*. Douglas & McIntyre, Distributed in the USA by Publishers Group West, 2003, RL 5.8, 164p
The story of 14-year-old Shauzia, who escaped from Kabul, Afghanistan and who is unhappy with her life as a refugee in a camp in Pakistan.

Holm, Anne, 1922. *I Am David*. Harcourt, 2004, 1965, RL 7.1, 239p
After escaping from an Eastern European concentration camp where he has spent most of his life, a 12-year-old boy struggles to cope with an entirely strange world as he flees northward to freedom in Denmark.

Laird, Elizabeth. *Kiss the Dust*. Puffin Books, 1994, 1991, IL or RL, 278p
Her father's involvement with the Kurdish resistance movement in Iraq forces thirteen-year-old Tara to flee with her family over the border into Iran, where they face an unknown future.

Mead, Alice. *Year of No Rain*. Farrar, Straus and Giroux, 2003, RL 5.1, 129p
In 1999, when rebel soldiers come to their village in southern Sudan, Stephen and his friends escape but hope to be able to return again.

Mikaelsen, Ben, 1952. *Red Midnight*. HarperTrophy/Rayo, 2003, 2002, RL 4.1, 212p
After soldiers kill his family, 12-year-old Santiago and his four-year-old sister flee Guatemala in a kayak and try to reach the United States.

Naidoo, Beverley. *The Other Side of Truth*. HarperCollins, 2001, RL 5.8, 252p
Smuggled out of Nigeria after their mother's murder, Sade and her younger brother are abandoned in London when their uncle fails to meet them at the airport. They are fearful of their new surroundings and of what may have happened to their journalist father back in Nigeria.

Shea, Pegi Deitz. *Tangled Threads: A Hmong Girl's Story*. Clarion Books, 2003, RL 8.0, 236p
After ten years in a refugee camp in Thailand, 13-year-old Mai Yang travels to Providence, Rhode Island, where her Americanized cousins introduce her to pizza, shopping, and beer, while her grandmother and new friends keep her connected to her Hmong heritage.

Zephaniah, Benjamin. *Refugee Boy*. Bloomsbury Children's Books, Distributed by St. Martin's Press, 2001, IL or RL, 291p
Fourteen-year-old Alem Kelo adjusts to life as a foster child seeking asylum in London, while his Eritrean mother and Ethiopian father work for peace between their homelands in Africa.

CHAPTER 3

Science

Ecology

e·col·o·gy

a. The science of the relationships between organisms and their environments.

b. The relationship between organisms and their environment.

The ecology of our world is often a very delicate balancing act. Many species of plants and animals are on the verge of disappearing completely because of man's intrusion of the natural environment. In this chapter, students will be reading novels that deal with our interaction with our environment.

 Sample Booktalk:

Hiaasen, Carl. *Hoot*. Alfred A. Knopf, Distributed by Random House, 2002, IL YA, 292p

Roy is the new kid. He's been the new kid before and he knows the drill. The local bully preys on him on the school bus. The kids at school don't socialize with him. He will get through this. But a new dimension has been added to the routine this time. One day, as Dana is harassing him on the bus, Roy notices a strange kid running beside the bus. The kid appears to be about Roy's age but he isn't wearing shoes. Now, Florida may have a relaxed dress code compared to Montana, but Roy is pretty sure they require shoes in school. But, the kid isn't at school that day. Or the next. Sensing a mystery, Roy sets out to find the running boy and learn his secret. Could it have anything to do with the strange goings-on at the construction site nearby? Alligators in the porta-potties? Snakes in the yard? And just what are those holes people keep stepping in.

What Species Am I?

Students will research plants and animals on the endangered species list. They will find a minimum of six facts about one of the plants or animals on the list. They will then create a "What Species Am I?" booklet.

Students will use a template to create the booklet. Booklet covers can be cut from construction paper or heavy stock paper. The template is glued onto the cover and then clues will be filled in the boxes as indicated. The clues must be verifiable facts. When all clues are written, the booklet is folded. The covers can be decorated if desired.

Ideas for using the booklets:

- Use in learning centers.
- Use for a class activity and have students record the answers on an answer sheet.
- Students can be timed and see how many answers they can get in a limited time.
- Use as an anchoring activity for students who complete work early.

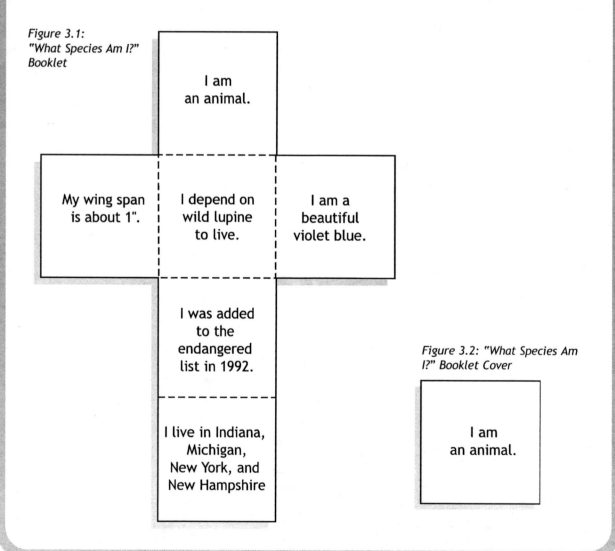

Figure 3.1: "What Species Am I?" Booklet

I am an animal.

My wing span is about 1".

I depend on wild lupine to live.

I am a beautiful violet blue.

I was added to the endangered list in 1992.

Figure 3.2: "What Species Am I?" Booklet Cover

I live in Indiana, Michigan, New York, and New Hampshire

I am an animal.

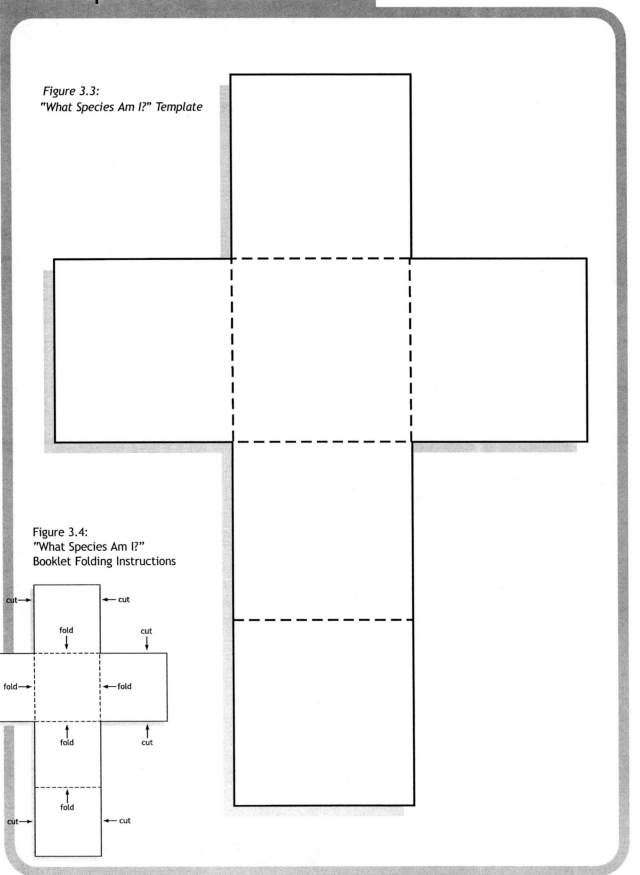

Figure 3.3:
"What Species Am I?" Template

Figure 3.4:
"What Species Am I?"
Booklet Folding Instructions

Ecology Book List

Bell, Hilari. *Songs of Power*. Hyperion, 2000, IL 5-8, RL 6.4, 219p
Someone is trying to sabotage the underwater habitat where Imina, the granddaughter of an Inuit shaman, lives after terrorists have infected the earth's food supply, and Imina must call on her still undeveloped magical skills to save the colony.

Cone, Molly. *Come Back, Salmon: How a Group of Dedicated Kids Adopted Pigeon Creek and Brought It Back to Life*. Sierra Club Books for Children, 1992, IL 3-6, RL 5.4, 48p
Describes the efforts of the Jackson Elementary School in Everett, Washington, to clean up a nearby stream, stock it with salmon, and preserve it as an unpolluted place where the salmon could return to spawn.

Crocker, Carter. *The Tale of the Swamp Rat*. Philomel Books, 2003, IL 5-8, RL 6.3, 232p
Guided by an ancient alligator, a silent young rat learns to find his own way in the drought-stricken swamp, despite having been orphaned under circumstances that sometimes cause other animals to reject him.

DeFelice, Cynthia C. *Lostman's River*. Avon Books, 1995, IL 5-8, RL 5.4, 156p
In the early 1900s, thirteen-year-old Tyler encounters vicious hunters whose actions threaten to destroy the Everglades ecosystem and, as a result, joins the battle to protect that fragile environment.

Doyle, Brian. *Spud Sweetgrass*. Douglas & McIntyre, Distributed in the USA by Publishers Group West, 1993, 1992, IL 5-8, RL 5.0, 139p
Spud Sweetgrass, a young man who sells french fries, sets out to find the culprit who is polluting his favorite beach by dumping grease into the Ottawa River.

George, Jean Craighead, 1919. *The Case of the Missing Cutthroats: An Eco Mystery*. HarperTrophy, 1999, IL 5-8, RL 3.5, 145p
After Spinner Shafter catches a cutthroat trout in the Snake River, she and her cousin Alligator search the nearby mountains to determine where the endangered fish came from and how it survived.

George, Jean Craighead, 1919. *The Fire Bug Connection: An Ecological Mystery*. HarperTrophy, 1995, IL 5-8, RL 4.7, 162p
Twelve-year-old Maggie receives European fire bugs for her birthday, but when they fail to metamorphose and explode instead, she uses scientific reasoning to determine the cause of their strange deaths.

Hayden, Torey L. *The Very Worst Thing*. HarperCollins, 2003, IL 5-8, RL 6.0, 169p
David has never had a permanent home or a real friend, but when he decides to try to hatch an owl egg with the help of a classmate, his life slowly begins to change for the better.

Hiaasen, Carl. *Hoot*. Alfred A. Knopf, Distributed by Random House, 2002, IL YA, 292p
Roy, who is new to his small Florida community, becomes involved in another boy's attempt to save a colony of burrowing owls from a proposed construction site.

Klass, David. *California Blue*. Scholastic, 1994, IL YA, RL 6.3, 199p
When 17-year-old John Rodgers discovers a new sub-species of butterfly, which may necessitate closing the mill where his dying father works, they find themselves on opposite sides of an environmental conflict.

Sleator, William. *The Beasties*. Dutton Children's Books, 1997, IL 5-8, RL 5.5, 198p
When 15-year-old Doug and his younger sister Colette move with their parents to a forested wilderness area, they encounter some weird creatures whose lives are endangered.

Wallace, Bill, 1947. *Blackwater Swamp*. Holiday House, 1994, IL 3-6, RL 4.9, 185p
Having discovered the true nature of the old woman known as the Witch of Blackwater Swamp, fifth grader Ted must decide whether to come to her aid when she is accused of the thefts plaguing his small Louisiana town.

❖ Medical Ethics ❖

C loning. Stem cell research. Organ transplants. These are just some of the medical breakthroughs we have seen over the past years. As marvelous as each new medical breakthrough seems, they are usually not without controversy. From animal testing to religious aspects, most new medicine comes with a downside. In this chapter, we will be looking at books dealing with some of these controversial topics.

 ### Sample Booktalk:

Werlin, Nancy. *Double Helix*. Dial Books, 2004, IL YA, 252p

Why would Dr. Wyatt want to see Eli? Sure Eli sent him an email but he was really drunk at the time and it was a mistake. And now he's been summoned by one of the foremost scientists in the world. When Dr. Wyatt offers Eli a job at Transgenics Lab, Eli begins to think there is more going on than he thought. His father begs him not to take the job but won't explain why. Eli knows that there is some connection between his mother and Dr. Wyatt but is assured it was business not personal. What could possibly be going on at Transgenics? And what does it have to do with Eli.

Medical Ethics Book List

Alcock, Vivien. *The Monster Garden*. Houghton Mifflin, 1998, IL 5-8, RL 5.1, 164p
Using a tissue sample she believes is from one of her father's experiments in genetic engineering, Frankie accidentally creates a baby monster, which begins to grow at an alarming rate.

Farmer, Nancy, 1941. *The House of the Scorpion*. Atheneum Books for Young Readers, 2002, IL 5-8, RL 6.3, 380p
In a future where humans despise clones, Matt enjoys special status as the young clone of El Patron, the 142-year-old leader of a corrupt drug empire nestled between Mexico and the United States.

Halam, Ann. *Dr. Franklin's Island*. Wendy Lamb Books, 2002, IL YA, 245p
When their plane crashes over the Pacific Ocean, three science students are left stranded on a tropical island and then imprisoned by a doctor who is performing horrifying experiments on humans involving the transfer of animal genes.

Medical Ethics Study

Students will create a PowerPoint presentation informing the class of the medical ethics portrayed in their independent reading book. Before the work begins, a storyboard should be created that outlines the presentation.

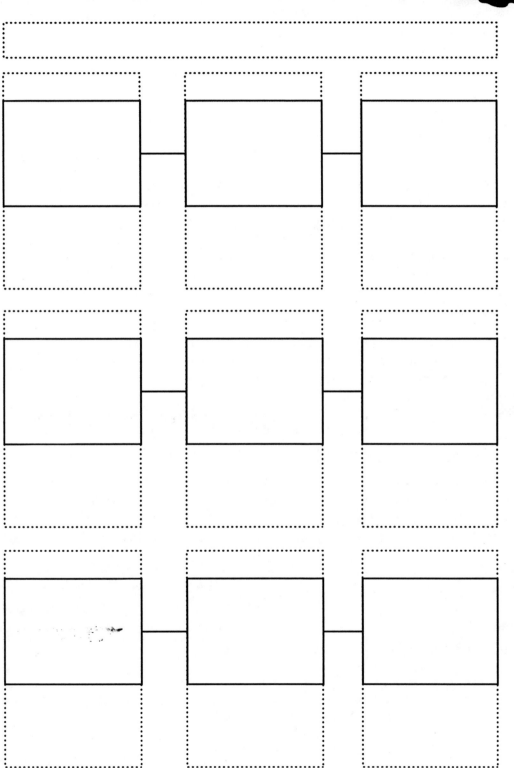

Figure 3.5: Medical Ethics Study Storyboard

Halam, Ann. *Taylor Five*. Wendy Lamb Books, 2004, IL 5-8, RL 6.7, 197p
Fourteen-year-old Taylor is still dealing with the fact that she is a clone produced by the same company that funds the Orangutan Reserve, which is her home on the island of Borneo, when the Reserve is attacked and she flees with her younger brother and Uncle, the Reserve's mascot.

Horowitz, Anthony, 1955. *Point Blank*. Philomel Books, 2002, 2001, IL 5-8, RL 8.3, 215p
Fourteen-year-old Alex continues his work as a spy for the British MI6, investigating an exclusive school for boys in the French Alps.

Kaye, Marilyn. *Pursuing Amy*. Bantam Books, 1998, IL 5-8, RL 7.5, 165p
Amy finds it difficult to hide her past and true identity from other people.

Kerner, Charlotte. *Blueprint*. Lerner Publications Company, 2000, IL YA, 189p
Siri Sellin, one of the first human clones, writes a bitter memoir of her childhood as the daughter of a famous and self-absorbed composer.

Lasky, Kathryn. *Star Split*. Hyperion Paperbacks for Children, 2001, 1999, IL 5-8, RL 6.0, 203p
In 3038, thirteen-year-old Darci uncovers an underground movement to save the human race from genetic enhancement technology.

Lorimer, Janet. *Bugged!* Saddleback, 2001, IL YA, RL 5.1, 76p
Twins Jean and Jared, dismayed about the changes taking place on their island home, decide to investigate when they come to suspect something shady is going on at the top-secret HybriGene laboratory.

Luiken, N. M. *Violet Eyes: A Novel*. Pocket Pulse, 2001, IL YA, 246p
Angel and Michael both have violet eyes and together they struggle to find their destiny against unknown, powerful enemies.

Roy, Ron, 1940. *Who Cloned the President?* Golden Books, 2001, IL 3-6, RL 2.8, 75p
KC discovers that the President of the United States has been replaced by a clone and sets out with her friend Marshall on a dangerous mission to set things right.

Skurzynski, Gloria. *The Clones*. Atheneum Books for Young Readers, 2002, IL 5-8, RL 5.8, 181p
Fifteen-year-old Corgan, having won the right to live on the Isles of Hiva for his role in winning the Virtual War along with teammates Sharla and Brig, soon finds himself raising the increasingly hostile clone of Brig, a young mutant genius, who died shortly after the war.

Watts, Peter. *Starfish*. Tor, 1999, IL YA, 317p
When an international corporation develops a power facility at the bottom of the ocean, they employ a bioengineered crew to man it, but it soon becomes apparent that although the crew can withstand the underwater environment, it makes them crazy, and the crew is capable of causing a deadly disaster.

Werlin, Nancy. *Double Helix*. Dial Books, 2004, IL YA, 252p
Eighteen-year-old Eli discovers a shocking secret about his life and his family while working for a Nobel Prize-winning scientist whose specialty is genetic engineering.

Food and Nutrition

The study of food and nutrition is a staple during the middle school years. Students learn what a healthy diet consists of and they learn the importance of maintaining a healthy lifestyle. In this chapter, we will be reading novels in which food or nutrition play a major role. The kids will just eat these up!

Sample Booktalk:

Creech, Sharon. *Granny Torrelli Makes Soup*. Joanna Cotler Books, 2003, IL 3-6, RL 4.5, 141p

Bailey and Rosie are best friends. They live next door to each other and were born just a week apart. They've always been as close as sister and brother--maybe closer because they chose each other. When Rosie found out that Bailey was legally blind, she started looking out for him even more. Now they are both 12-years-old and are still best friends. When they have a fight, they find comfort and wisdom while helping out Granny Torrelli in the kitchen. Join them as they enjoy pasta and family stories while Granny Torrelli Makes Soup.

Food and Nutrition Book List

Bauer, Joan, 1951. *Hope Was Here*. G.P. Putnam's Sons, 2000, IL YA, 186p
When 16-year-old Hope and the aunt who has raised her move from Brooklyn to Mulhoney, Wisconsin, to work as waitress and cook in the Welcome Stairways diner, they become involved with the diner owner's political campaign to oust the town's corrupt mayor.

Clark, Catherine. *Truth or Dairy*. Harper Tempest, 2000, IL YA, 268p
Courtney, a Colorado high school senior, becomes the bane of her friends' and family's existence as she fumes over being dumped by her college-bound boyfriend--but a temptation named Grant may be enough to drag her back into happiness.

Creech, Sharon. *Granny Torrelli Makes Soup*. Joanna Cotler Books, 2003, IL 3-6, RL 4.5, 141p
With the help of her wise old grandmother, 12-year-old Rosie manages to work out some problems in her relationship with her best friend, Bailey, the boy next door.

Dahl, Roald. *James and the Giant Peach: A Children's Story*. Knopf, Distributed by Random House, 1996, IL 3-6, RL 5.6, 126p
Fantasy about a young boy and a huge magical peach.

Healthy Decisions

1. The Food Pyramid:
   <http://www.schoolmenu.com/New/spotlight1.htm>.
   Write down 10 interesting facts about the food pyramid.

2. Build a Nutritional Meal and Balance Your Diet:
   <http://exhibits.pacsci.org/nutrition/cafe/cafe.html>
   Build a meal and see if it provides the goodness that you need. Examine your diet. Do you eat at least five servings a day of fruits and vegetables? How might you change your diet to ensure that you eat from all of the five main food groups?

3. A Guide to Daily Food Choices:
   <http://schoolmeals.nal.usda.gov/py/pmap1.gif>
   Use the Pyramid to help you eat better every day--the Dietary Guidelines way.

4. Food Riddles:
   <http://www2.lhric.org/pocantico/nutrition/nutrition.html>
   Which foods are good for you? Why? Learn about the food groups. Why do we need to eat a balanced diet?

5. Student Research Activity—Nutrition and Diet Quiz:
   <http://www.enchantedlearning.com/classroom/quiz/nutrition.shtml>
   Introduction to research on the Internet—nutrition and diet quiz.

6. Food Pyramid Quiz:
   <http://www.enchantedlearning.com/food/foodpyramidquiz.shtml>
   Can you answer these questions about healthy eating?

7. The Human Body's Digestive System:
   <http://yucky.kids.discovery.com/noflash/body/pg000126.html>
   What is the purpose of the digestive system? Are teeth important in this system? After the food is swallowed what path does it take? Describe the journey which food takes after it enters the mouth.

Haduch, Bill. *Food Rules!: The Stuff You Munch, Its Crunch, Its Punch, and Why You Sometimes Lose Your Lunch*. Dutton Children's Books, 2001, IL 3-6, RL 5.0, 106p
A lighthearted look at how the digestive system works that also contains food facts such as what comprised the last meal on the "Titanic."

Hardman, Ric Lynden. *Sunshine Rider: The First Vegetarian Western*. Delacorte Press, 1998. IL YA, 343p
In the late 1800s while on a cattle drive that takes him north from Texas, 17-year-old Wylie learns that it is no longer necessary to run from the father he never knew. But what happens when Wylie, who has been hired as the assistant cook, goes vegetarian?

Horvath, Polly. *Everything on a Waffle*. Farrar, Straus and Giroux, 2001, IL 5-8, RL 5.9, 149p
Eleven-year-old Primrose, who lives in a small fishing village in British Columbia, recounts her experiences and all that she learns about human nature and the unpredictability of life in the months after her parents are lost at sea.

Rocklin, Joanne. *Strudel Stories*. Delacorte Press, 1999, IL 3-6, RL 3.5, 131p
Seven generations of a Jewish family hear stories of their family history, all told while making apple strudel.

Rockwell, Thomas, 1933. *How to Eat Fried Worms*. F. Watts, 1973, IL 3-6, RL 4.2, 115p
Two boys set out to prove that worms can make a delicious meal.

Shaw, Tucker. *Flavor of the Week*. Hyperion, 2003, IL YA, 220p
Cyril, an overweight boy who is good friends with Rose but wishes he could be more, helps his best friend Nick woo her with culinary masterpieces which Cyril himself secretly creates. Includes recipes from the story.

Smith, Robert Kimmel, 1930. *Chocolate Fever*. Putnam's, 1989, 1972, IL 3-6, RL 4.8, 93p
From eating too much chocolate, Henry breaks out in brown bumps that help him foil some hijackers and teach him a valuable lesson about self-indulgence.

Natural Disasters

Floods, hurricanes, earthquakes. The stuff of Hollywood movies. These natural disasters make for good books as well. But what part is real and what part imaginary? In this section, we will read books where Mother Nature is the main character.

 ## Sample Booktalk:

Hobbs, Will. *Wild Man Island*. HarperCollins, 2002, IL 5-8, RL 7.1, 184p

Fourteen-year-old Andy Galloway is on a trip of a lifetime. He is on a sea-kayaking trip in Alaska. He has dreamed of doing this for a long time. He's picked this particular sea adventure because it will bring him close to Hidden Falls. That's where his father died many years ago. His father was an archaeologist doing research on primitive people. He believed that there were people living in Alaska long before the landbridge developed that allowed people from Asia to cross over. He believed that people used primitive boats to get to Alaska long before that. He was attempting to get proof of that when he was killed in an accident. And now Andy finds himself only a few miles from where his father died. Should he try to sneak away from the group and go out on his own? Andy knows that's dangerous. But, it's so close. What could possibly go wrong?

Natural Disasters Book List

Bodett, Tom. *Williwaw!* Dell Yearling, 2000, 1999, IL 5-8, RL 5.9, 192p
In their father's absence, 13-year-old September and her younger brother Ivan disobey his orders by taking the boat out on their Alaska bay, where they are caught in a terrifying storm called a Williwaw.

Carbone, Elisa Lynn. *Storm Warriors*. Alfred A. Knopf, Distributed by Random House, 2001, IL 5-8, RL 6.5, 168p
In 1895, after his mother's death, 12-year-old Nathan moves with his father and grandfather to Pea Island off the coast of North Carolina, where he hopes to join the all-black crew at the nearby lifesaving station, despite his father's objections.

Natural Disasters

Using the novel as a starting point, students will investigate the natural hazard from the book and select one of the following activities to complete.

Verbal

Students will introduce natural hazards or disasters and discuss types and causes.

Logical

Students will identify locations and occurrences of natural hazards or disasters. Students will identify locations that are susceptible to particular hazards or disasters and discuss procedures to follow during the disaster.

Visual

Students will collect images and text to identify a natural hazard or disaster.

Musical

Students will explore sound clips that identify a natural hazard or disaster. Students will find and provide sound to be used while presenting their report.

Interpersonal

Students will identify possible rescue operations in the event of a disaster.

Intrapersonal

Students will locate information discussing how individuals have survived a natural hazard or disaster, thereby easing their fears in the event of a disaster.

Kinesthetic

Students will perform simple experiments if available for the purpose of demonstrating a disaster, for example, a volcanic eruption or tornado.

Naturalist

Students will discuss how to prepare for a disaster and possible ways to prevent a disaster from occurring.

Existentialist

Students will discuss the impact a natural hazard or disaster has on society as well as the global community. They will identify lessons learned as a result of a disaster.

Duey, Kathleen. *Blizzard, Estes Park, Colorado, 1886*. Aladdin Paperbacks, 1998, IL 3-6, RL 5.2, 159p
When 12-year-old Maggie attempts to rescue Hadyn during a sudden blizzard in the Colorado mountains in 1886, both cousins change their minds about each other.

Hobbs, Will. *Wild Man Island*. HarperCollins, 2002, IL 5-8, RL 7.1, 184p
After 14-year-old Andy slips away from his kayaking group to visit the wilderness site of his archaeologist father's death, a storm strands him on Admiralty Island, Alaska, where he manages to survive, encounters unexpected animal and human inhabitants, and looks for traces of the earliest prehistoric immigrants to America.

Kehret, Peg. *Escaping the Giant Wave*. Simon & Schuster Books for Young Readers, 2003, IL 3-6, RL 5.9, 151p
When an earthquake creates a tsunami while 13-year-old Kyle is babysitting his sister during a family vacation at a Pacific Coast resort, he tries to save himself, his sister, and a boy who has bullied him for years. Includes an author's note that provides factual information on tsunamis.

Kehret, Peg. *The Volcano Disaster*. Pocket Books, 1998, IL 5-8, RL 4.8, 136p
Warren and Betsy are accidentally transported back to the eruption of the Mt. St. Helens volcano in 1980.

Naylor, Phyllis Reynolds. *Blizzard's Wake*. Atheneum Books for Young Readers, 2002, IL YA, 212p
In March of 1941, when a severe blizzard suddenly hits Bismarck, North Dakota, a girl trying to save her stranded father and brother inadvertently helps the man who killed her mother four years before.

Parkinson, Curtis. *Storm-Blast*. Tundra Books of Northern New York, 2003, IL 5-8, RL 6.2, 156p
Regan, his sister Carol, and their cousin Matt struggle for survival after a storm leaves them stranded in a dinghy far out at sea.

Petersen, P. J. *Rising Water*. Simon & Schuster Books for Young Readers, 2002, IL 5-8, RL 6.7, 120p
Tracy, her brother, and the new animal care volunteer at the Jefferson Science Center travel by boat to feed a dog stranded by flooding, and end up having a full day of dangerous adventures, which give them new perspectives about themselves and about each other.

Thompson, Kate. *Switchers*. Hyperion Paperbacks for Children, 1999, 1998, IL 5-8, RL 5.5, 220p
When freakish weather grips the Arctic regions and moves southward, an Irish girl and her strange companion save the world from disaster through their ability to switch into animal forms.

CHAPTER 4

Overall Middle School Years

Coming of Age

Is there any more of a relevant topic for middle schoolers than books about growing up? This is a time in their lives when massive changes occur and they are struggling to understand themselves and to learn that they are not alone. Novels that take a character through this time are sure to be a hit with students. In this chapter, we look at coming of age from a variety of viewpoints.

Sample Booktalk:

Brashares, Ann. *The Sisterhood of the Traveling Pants*. Delacorte, 2001, IL YA, RL 6.8, 294p

Lena, Tibby, Bridget, and Carmen have been best friends all their lives. Well, actually, they've been friends since before they were born. You see, their mothers were in birth class together and the girls were all born a few weeks apart. As the years went by, the mothers drifted apart but the girls remained friends. This summer will see them separate for the first time. Lena will be going to Greece to stay with her Grandmother. Bridget is going to soccer camp in Baja California. Carmen is going to visit her Dad in South Carolina. And Tibby is staying home. As the girls spend their last night together, they notice an old pair of jeans that Carmen bought in a thrift store. As each girl tries on the jeans, they note a bit of magic. Even though the girls are different sizes and shapes, the jeans seem to fit them each perfectly. They must be magic! The girls decide that the jeans need to travel between the girls during the summer and carry their stories to each other. Follow the girls' adventures as they tell their stories to the Sisterhood of the Traveling Pants.

Graffiti Poster

Using the main character from the book, create a graffiti poster that helps others understand the character. The poster should include drawings, quotes, likes, and dislikes.

Figure 4.1: Graffiti Poster

Brashares, Ann. *The Sisterhood of the Traveling Pants.*
Delacorte, 2001.

Coming of Age Book List

Anderson, Laurie Halse. *Speak*. Puffin, 2001, 1999, IL YA, 197p
A traumatic event near the end of the summer has a devastating effect on Melinda's freshman
year in high school.

Brashares, Ann. *The Sisterhood of the Traveling Pants*. Delacorte, 2001, IL YA, RL 6.8, 294p
Carmen decides to discard an old pair of jeans, but Tibby, Lena, and Bridget think they are
great and decide that whoever the pants fit best will get them. When the jeans fit everyone
perfectly, a sisterhood and a memorable summer begin.

McKay, Hilary. *Saffy's Angel*. Margaret K. McElderry Books, 2002, IL 3-6, RL 6.5, 152p
After learning that she was adopted, 13-year-old Saffron's relationship with her eccentric,
artistic family changes, until they help her go back to Italy where she was born to find a
special memento of her past.

Mikaelsen, Ben, 1952. *Touching Spirit Bear*. HarperCollins, 2001, IL 5-8, RL 6.7, 241p
After his anger erupts into violence, 15-year-old Cole, in order to avoid going to prison, agrees
to participate in a sentencing alternative based on the Native American Circle Justice, and he
is sent to a remote Alaskan Island where an encounter with a huge Spirit Bear changes his life.

Oates, Joyce Carol, 1938. *Big Mouth & Ugly Girl*. HarperTempest, 2002, IL YA, 266p
When 16-year-old Matt is falsely accused of threatening to blow up his high school and his friends turn against him, an unlikely classmate comes to his aid.

Paulsen, Gary. *The Beet Fields: Memories of a Sixteenth Summer*. Delacorte Press, 2000, IL YA, 160p
A boy runs away from home and his drunken parents and spends his 16th summer learning about life as a migrant laborer and carnival worker.

Paulsen, Gary. *Guts: The True Stories Behind Hatchet and the Brian Books*. Delacorte Press, 2001, IL 5-8, RL 5.4, 148p
The author relates incidents in his life and how they inspired parts of his books about the character, Brian Robeson.

Powell, Randy. *Three Clams and an Oyster*. Farrar, Straus and Giroux, 2002, IL YA, 216p
During their humorous search to find a fourth player for their flag football team, three high school juniors are forced to examine their long friendship, their individual flaws, and their inability to try new experiences.

Sones, Sonya. *What My Mother Doesn't Know*. Simon & Schuster Books for Young Readers, 2001, IL YA, 259p
Sophie describes her relationships with a series of boys as she searches for Mr. Right.

Spinelli, Jerry. *Loser*. Joanna Cotler Books, 2002, IL 3-6, RL 5.2, 218p
Even though his classmates from first grade on have considered him strange and a loser, Daniel Zinkoff's optimism and exuberance and the support of his loving family do not allow him to feel that way about himself.

Wolff, Virginia Euwer. *True Believer*. Atheneum Books for Young Readers, 2001, IL YA, 264p
Living in the inner city amidst guns and poverty, 15-year-old LaVaughn learns from old and new friends, and inspiring mentors, that life is what you make it--an occasion to rise to.

✸ Index ✸

G

Gaeddert, LouAnn Bigge. *Friends and Enemies*, 73

Gaines, Ernest J, 1933. *The Autobiography of Miss Jane Pittman*, 62, 77

Garlock, Dorothy. *With Hope*, 63

Garvie, Maureen. *George Johnson's War*, 47

Gellis, Roberta. *Bull God*, 36

George, Jean Craighead, 1919. *The Case of the Missing Cutthroats: An Eco Mystery*, 86

George, Jean Craighead, 1919. *The Fire Bug Connection : An Ecological Mystery*, 86

Giff, Patricia Reilly. *Lily's Crossing*, 73

Glenn, Mel. *Jump Ball: A Basketball Season in Poems*, 11

Glenn, Mel. *Who Killed Mr. Chippendale?: A Mystery in Poems*, 11

Golding, William, 1911. *Lord of the Flies*, 30

Goodman, Joan E. *Peregrine*, 41

Graffiti Poster, 99

Grassby, Donna. *A Seaside Alphabet*, 5

Great Depression, 63

Great Depression Book List, 63

Greek Mythology, 35

Greek Mythology Fiction Book List, 36

Gregory, Kristiana. *A Journey of Faith*, 57

Gregory, Kristiana. *Cleopatra VII: Daughter of the Nile*, 34

Gregory, Kristiana. *Seeds of Hope: The Gold Rush Diary of Susanna Fairchild*, 57

Grimes, Nikki. *Bronx Masquerade*, 11

Grimes, Nikki. *C Is foFor City*, 5

Guzman, Lila, 1952. *Lorenzo's Secret Mission*, 47

H

Haahr, Berit I. *The Minstrel's Tale*, 41

Haddix, Margaret Peterson. *Among the Hidden*, 30

Haduch, Bill. *Food Rules!: The Stuff You Munch, Its Crunch, Its Punch, and Why You Sometimes Lose Your Lunch*, 93

Hahn, Mary Downing. *Hear the Wind Blow*, 49

Halam, Ann. *Dr. Franklin's Island*, 88

Halam, Ann. *Taylor Five*, 90

Hantman, Clea. *Heaven Sent*, 36

Hantman, Clea. *Love or Fate*, 37

Hantman, Clea. *Muses on the Move*, 37

Hantman, Clea. *Three Girls and a God*, 37

Hardman, Ric Lynden. *Sunshine Rider: The First Vegetarian Western*, 93

Harley, Bill, 1954. *Sarah's Story*, 18

Harlow, Joan Hiatt. *Shadows on the Sea*, 73

Haseley, Dennis. *The Amazing Thinking Machine*, 65

Hausman, Gerald. *Tom Cringle: Battle on the High Seas*, 42

Hayden, Torey L. *The Very Worst Thing*, 86

Healthy Decisions, 92

Herman, John, 1944. *Labyrinth*, 37

Hermes, Patricia. *A Perfect Place*, 57

Hermes, Patricia. *Westward to Home*, 57

Herschler, Mildred Barger. *The Darkest Corner*, 77

Hesse, Karen. *Out of the Dust*, 11

Hiaasen, Carl. *Hoot*, 83, 86

Hite, Sid. *The Journal of Rufus Rowe: A Witness to the Battle of Fredericksburg*, 49

Hobbs, Will. *Wild Man Island*, 96

Holm, Anne, 1922. *I am David*, 79

Holm, Jennifer L. *Boston Jane: An Adventure*, 55, 57

Holocaust, 66

Holocaust Book List, 66

Holocaust Investigation, 67

Hoobler, Dorothy. *The Second Decade: Voyages*, 62

Horowitz, Anthony, 1955. *Point Blank*, 90

Horvath, Polly. *Everything on a Waffle*, 93

Hughes, Pat (Patrice Raccio) *Guerrilla Season*, 48

Hunt, Angela Elwell, 1957. *Dreamers*, 34

Huxley, Aldous, 1894-1963. *Brave New World*, 30

I

I Am Poem, 10

Ingold, Jeanette. *Mountain Solo*, 57

Interpreting Wordless Picture Books, 7

Isaacs, Anne. *Torn Thread*, 66

Isadora, Rachel. *On Your Toes: A Ballet A B C*, 5

It's Time To Go—Pack Your Bags, 79

J

Jacq, Christian. *Nefer the Silent. Volume I*, 34

Jacques, Brian. The Angel's Command : A Tale from the Castaways of the Flying Dutchman, 44

About the Author

Nancy J. Keane is a school librarian in New Hampshire. She has been a lover a children's literature all her life, so working with books and children is a perfect match for her. In addition to her work in the school, Nancy also hosts a television show on local television. *Kids Book Beat* is a monthly show that features children from the area booktalking their favorite books. The show also features local authors and storytellers. Nancy has also authored a children's fiction book and several books on using booktalks.

Nancy is the author of an award winning Web site Booktalks--Quick and Simple (http://www.nancykeane.com/booktalks). The site logs about 20,000 hits a day and has proven to be indispensable to librarians and teachers. The database includes more than 1,500 ready-to-use booktalks, and contributions are welcome from educators. Additionally, Nancy has a page of thematic booklists available on her page. ATN Book Lists consists of about 900 thematic lists culled from suggestions from several professional email discussion lists.

Nancy received a B.A. in child psychology from the University of Massachusetts, Amherst, an M.L.S. from University of Rhode Island, and an M.A. in Educational Technology from George Washington University. She is an adjunct faculty member at New Hampshire Technical College, Connected University, and teaches workshops for the University of New Hampshire.

Nancy lives in Concord, New Hampshire with her son Alex. They share their home with their dog and four cats. Her daughter, son-in-law, and precious new grandson, Aiden, live nearby.